VEGETARIAN CHILDREN

Also by Sharon K. Yntema

Vegetarian Baby

VEGETARIAN CHILDREN

A SUPPORTIVE GUIDE FOR PARENTS

SHARON K. YNTEMA

ILLUSTRATIONS BY
DIANA SOUZA

McBooks Press

The author and publisher believe that this book outlines an excellent regi-men for raising a healthy child. However, they cannot accept any respon-sibility for the health of your child should any problems arise. Every child has individual nutritional needs. While using the information in this book, you should consult with your pediatrician or public health nurse about your child's individual requirements.

Cover design by Diana Souza
Book design by Mary A. Scott
Typesetting by Bets Ltd.

Library of Congress Cataloging-in-Publication Data

Yntema, Sharon, 1951-
    Vegetarian children

    Bibliography: p.
    Includes index
    1. Vegetarian children   2. Vegetarianism—
Social aspects.   3. Child development.   I. Title
RJ216.Y575   1987   649'.3   87-61183
ISBN 0-935526-13-7 (lib. bdg.)
ISBN 0-935526-14-5 (pbk.)

This book is distributed to the book and natural food trades by several small press wholesalers and by McBooks Press, 908 Steam Mill Road, Ithaca, NY 14850. Individuals may order this book through bookstores or directly from McBooks Press. Please include $1.35 postage and handling with mail orders. In New York State please add $.82 sales tax.

Printed in the United States of America

9 8 7 6 5 4 3

For Nikolas and Marcia

Thanks

A special thank you to Karen Schantz, Diana Souza, Mary Brown, Alex Skutt, Mary Scott, William Kehoe, Katharyn Aal, Leonard Rifas, Kathy Rodgers, Billy Kaupe, and all the vegetarian parents who gave me ideas through letters, conversations and interviews.

About the Author

Sharon Kathryn Yntema was born in Detroit in 1951. She grew up in the US Virgin Islands, where her mother first introduced her to a vegetarian diet. She received a B.A. in Psychology from Earlham College and an M.A. in Early Childhood Special Education from George Washington University. Before her son was born in 1978, Ms. Yntema worked as a child development specialist at the Day Care and Child Development Council of Tompkins County in Ithaca, New York. She continues to make her home in Ithaca, where she has worked for several years as a technical writer and is currently studying accounting and ancient Greek. Her nieces and nephews join her son in their enjoyment of life as healthy vegetarian children.

Table of Contents

Editors' note on the use of gender pronouns in this book: After experimenting with several different non-sexist formulations ("he or she," "he/she," "s/he") and finding them cumbersome or ugly, we decided to use "she" and "he" alternately by chapter.

Introduction

Raising a child on a healthy vegetarian diet is one of the most concrete actions of love a parent can make. On a physical level, exposure to healthy foods allows optimal growth and helps prevent disease. On a social level, following a healthy vegetarian diet is a basic step toward increasing the chance that our planet will survive and flourish.

Vegetarianism is, for me, the ideal parenting medium. It allows me to nurture a healthy child and instill him with important social values. The concept of connection between all living things is essential to vegetarianism. It leads me to a continuing interaction with others, widening my own knowledge of the world which I then share with my son.

I try to accept the differences among vegetarians and am willing to consider openly new information or ideas that I had never encountered before. One advantage to being a parent is that parenting is a process, not something that is ruined or created in one day. As my understanding of vegetarianism deepens, my ability to relate in a healthy way to my family, and to the world at large, also grows.

When I was the parent of a baby, I needed good nutritional information about feeding a vegetarian infant. At that time, all that existed in print on this subject was short passages in books intended for adults who were choosing vegetarianism. Many targeted readers were not even considering having children yet and were more concerned with establishing healthy vegetarian eating habits for themselves. My first book, *Vegetarian Baby*, was designed to support what I perceived as a slowly growing population of new vegetarian parents, by presenting practical information on nutrition and physical development of very young children.

Now I am the parent of a vegetarian child who has a much wider variety of needs. No longer can I prepare healthy meals without considering his likes and dislikes, his peers' opinions, and his attitudes toward food in general. I live with a give and take with this young person who had once happily eaten any food I offered. Issues of food, nutrition, and feeding now have an ambiguity that makes "right" answers less obvious and maybe impossible.

Parenting is a complex set of responsibilities in which diet plays a relatively smaller role as the child becomes more independent. From the infant stage, when feeding is central to most interactions, parents must adjust to a relationship in which friends, television, and school take up the majority of a child's time.

How can I hope to have a final say in what my son eats when he spends the night with a friend? How can I make sure he eats what I give him for lunch? Does he know why he is a vegetarian? What is a proper response to the statement, "Sometimes I wish I liked hot dogs so that I could be like the other guys at the baseball game"? What can I say when he ridicules another child for eating meat?

Many unanswered questions arise, not only for vegetarian parents, but for every parent. In this spirit, *Vegetarian Children* presents information in many areas of normal development, with special consideration to a vegetarian lifestyle.

I have included discussions of the physical, social, and psychological development of the vegetarian child as well as an introduction to some of the moral questions that these children and their parents may face. Because there has been a change in the results of research regarding vegetarian children, I have added an historical overview of this data, which begins in the early 1970's with a gloomy outlook, but turns more optimistic as nutritional information becomes more available to vegetarian parents in the 1980's.

In frustration, one parent told me, "It seems that you have to educate your child to be an intelligent consumer when she is 3 months old." This condition feels true when a parent considers all the pressure toward junk food in the supermarket, on television, and in the homes of relatives and friends. Cultural trends that fight against a healthy diet eventually invade even the most protected family atmosphere. Parents who exclude all junk food and television from their homes may still find that their child knows brand names of candy bars at a relatively early age.

Vegetarian Children explores the effects of peer pressure on children, and ways in which parents can help counteract the dominance of a meat-eating, sugar-coated society. Parents need to realize that while *they* may be easily able to withstand teasing about their choice to be vegetarians, children will have a much harder time. In fact, research suggests that parents who are too strict, without regard to the child's need for social acceptance, may inadvertently discourage their child from healthy eating attitudes as she becomes more independent. Although the change may be hard to accept, the complete control one has over an infant's diet is not realistic as the baby gets older. It therefore seems better to offer support, encouragement, and, most important, good role modeling.

Parents will rely on their own moral values as they respond to many of the difficulties of food choice and child-rearing that may arise within the home, the community, and the world at large. How these values are transmitted to the child and how the child internalizes them is a process that takes place over a long period of time, not within weeks or even a couple of years. Parents must remember that values can develop and mature over a lifetime. A chapter in *Vegetarian Children* devoted to a discussion of moral development takes into account the theories of Piaget, Kohlberg, and Gilligan, in an attempt to apply their ideas to practical everyday life.

Raising a vegetarian baby is usually centered around home life, since a baby needs mostly to eat, sleep, and become familiar with a loving environment. Raising a vegetarian child, however, exposes parents and children to a culture that standardizes meat eating and other unhealthy nutritional choices. If a parent stays involved only in the home, and refuses to confront the realities of a less than ideal world, the child will have to face them alone.

For parents, resolving to become vegetarians was probably a life-affirming decision. Many experienced the minority status of vegetarianism in the 1970's as an empowering choice, an identification with a group of people with similar values. It is important for parents to continue their ties with this community, for the emotional and physical health of the whole family. If vegetarian parents provide rituals, such as a vegetarian solstice celebration with other families, their children will know they are not so alone and different as they might seem in the normal public school environment, for example.

Vegetarianism is much more than not eating meat. It can be explored to greater depths depending upon a parent's time, inclination, and resources. To be a vegetarian means, at the very least, to look at one's personal life situation and to perceive how it relates to the surrounding culture. A child is sure to be asked, "Why are you a vegetarian?" and just as surely to ask the same question of herself and her family.

As a child grows older, a parent can answer this question with increasing detail, just as one would provide different answers to questions about sex to a three-year-old than to a nine-year-old. Parents need to keep in mind that their children have not truly chosen to be vegetarians, especially when they were brought up that way from birth. But if parents and children talk with each other and discuss some of the many reasons for becoming vegetarians, the child will be more likely to choose vegetarianism on her own despite outside influences.

The resources available to each parent for dealing with vegetarianism will vary, just as every vegetarian parent experiences his or her role differently. For some, finding healthy food means the inconvenience of placing mail orders or facing a barrage of disapproving relatives. For others, a vegetarian life may be easier if a vegetarian community exists where the family lives. Health food stores and local organic food producers will often be able to help parents find any extra information they may need. Libraries are usually willing to order at least some books on vegetarianism, and preschools and day-care centers are usually receptive to parent involvement in providing early exposure to healthy foods.

Vegetarianism has tremendous potential for connecting scattered social issues, and can expose children and parents to the problems of animal rights, politics of big business, natural foods, changing local communities, protecting the environment, and the health of our own bodies. In *Vegetarian Children*, I have provided some ideas and resources for parents who are interested in pursuing any of these related issues.

In writing this book, I have felt how easily everything can be linked in some way to vegetarianism; personal health is not separate from the health and future of our world. Interrelatedness is the natural structure of the living world, and raising healthy vegetarian children is a vital link to a well future for us all.

CHILD DEVELOPMENT 1

B eyond being necessary for survival, eating is a part of life endowed with tremendous emotional significance. For the very young child, being fed and being touched happen at the same time. Hunger pains are often assuaged while babies are being held in loving arms. However, as children grow older, eating does not continue in this simple, positive relationship to emotions.

When a baby is weaned and parents can no longer rely on the ideal nourishment that nursing provides, concern over the child's eating habits is likely to increase. And when a baby is switched from a feeding-on-demand schedule to one that takes into account the needs of the rest of the family, feeding becomes more complicated. A problem arises when a child is not hungry at the time meals are being served, or hungry when they are not. If a child wants to eat only certain foods, or likes to eat tremendous amounts of food sometimes and nothing at all at other times, or if he displays annoying table manners or complains about what is served, then adverse emotional reactions to eating begin to develop.

Naturally, eating and food assume an emotional significance. Because food satisfies such a basic need so frequently, it inevitably affects us all in very powerful ways. Rather than denying or fighting this connection, we can try to understand any sources of conflict whenever possible. By looking at children's development in relation to food, one can put the behavior of a particular child into perspective. Once a child's natural skills and tendencies for healthy eating are understood, they can be incorporated into the eating style and habits of the family.

The development of eating preferences and behaviors in young children is both idiosyncratic and patterned. Three factors operate during this process: taste preference, eating behavior, and emotional development. Taste preference includes such elements as texture and flavor. Eating behavior is a combination of the physiological and social responses to the food offered. Emotional development involves the deeply rooted connection between food and emotions that seems to exist in all societies.

In societies where food is not plentiful, taste preferences are not as obvious. Children rarely refuse a food, because (1) the food is probably familiar and (2) it is likely to be all the child will be offered to eat. In the United States and other more "developed" societies, most children have some pronounced food likes and dislikes. Food preference is important because it greatly determines what a child will actually eat. The "right" food does no good, and will not fulfill the child's Recommended Dietary Allowances, if he only looks grudgingly at it on his plate.

Eating behaviors are the responses a child gives when offered food. At first they are determined by physical capabilities, and later modified by the expectations of parents and by the child's emotional development. Very few children have stable eating habits. While this instability may be difficult for parents, it also may provide perspective: any behavior may be related to physical growth needs, may be experimental, and may change. Within the fluctuation of children's eating habits exist overall patterns of the development of the interrelationship of food and emotions.

The Gesell Institute of Child Development has been a major force for many years in observing and documenting child development patterns. Their expertise, combined with the research of other child development specialists, provides a sound description of changes in children's eating habits. The information on the following pages is drawn from these sources as well as my own observations.

Babies

The first year of life is one of tremendous physical growth for which a high-nutritive intake is essential. Babies under eight or nine months cannot tolerate an unhealthy diet. A good diet is so closely tied to normal development at this point in life that undernourishment usually shows up quickly. Fortunately, most parents naturally desire to offer the healthiest diet possible to their babies, but grandparents and friends may need to be discouraged from giving sweets and other unhealthy snacks.

The child's need to eat a great deal results in a willingness to eat almost anything offered. Although taste buds are present at birth, strong preferences do not appear until seven or eight months of age, and even then most parents find that babies are not especially choosy about foods they eat. This indifference often lasts through the child's first year.

The lack of strong food preferences at this point is suited for optimal development. Variety in foods offered exposes children to a wide range of nutrients, and this exposure forms the basis for a healthy diet. At this time parents should familiarize their children with many kinds of foods, since preference, as it begins to occur, is largely based on familiarity. Always, of course, parents should introduce new foods carefully and be alert to any signs of allergy.

Toddlers

When a child is weaned, his eating schedule is usually adapted to that of the rest of the family. Until he is about three years of age, problems at mealtimes usually center around manners rather than diet. In these very early years, parents have much control over the child's diet, so that he is less likely to fill up on "junk" food between meals or eat unbalanced meals.

A child over a year old begins to walk and talk, and develops taste preferences at the same time. According to studies by Dr. Diana Spillman of Florida State University, children have more taste buds in more places than adults—not only on the tongue, but also on the lips and on the inside of the mouth. These extra taste buds which are lost around age five, may explain why young children tend to stuff their mouths, despite adults' disapproval: a child can taste with more of his mouth!

1 ½ years   Although most children can eat by themselves by this age, they still do not have the bodily control that would assure socially acceptable table behavior. Reactions to these limitations vary from culture to culture. Among the Rajputs of Khalapur, India, a mother will feed her child until he is three or four. This Indian culture places importance upon eating without interruption; food left on a plate is considered to be polluted and should not be eaten. In Taira, an Okinawan village in Japan, young children are encouraged to eat properly with praise and attention from all the family. The child has chopsticks placed in his hand at each meal, even though he is still fed by an adult as part of a learning process in which he is not hurried or scolded.

2 years   The two-year-old continues to need help with feeding and is likely to play with food and dawdle at meals. He will probably refuse disliked foods and go on "food jags," preferring one food over all others for days or longer at a time.

Two-year-olds are notorious for their tendency to say "no"—a natural response, for a child of this age may often be hearing "no" as he explores his environment and goes out of bounds. Being able to say "no" himself is one of his first ways of obtaining power. Of course, refusal can be more than just an exercise of will. Children from one to three grow more slowly than before and thus have decreased appetites, although they continue to need more nutrients for their size than do adults.

Preschoolers

Parents' major focus with preschoolers is teaching manners so that the family can eat comfortably together. A regular chair may replace a high chair, and the child begins to eat with some self-control.

3 years The three-year-old, beginning to see mealtimes as a ritual, likes to set the table. Usually he can feed himself well, but still tends to scatter crumbs on the floor. At this age, a child either eats or talks; language ability has increased dramatically, and talking seems to be as interesting an activity as eating. Food dislikes are rarer now. Pleasing one's parents is strong motivation for good behavior at this age, and the child is generally cooperative.

Most children now will choose food based upon *familiarity* with it. According to a 1979 study by L. L. Birch, familiarity is a stronger factor for three-year-olds than even the sweetness of the food. This revelation may come as a surprise to some parents. Others, who proudly point to a child who seems not to have a sweet tooth, may find a year later that the story is quite different, for at about age four *sweetness* becomes the primary factor in a child's food choice.

3 1/2 years   At this age, children are full of "Why? How? What? When?" questions, not necessarily related to the food on hand. Unlike in the months preceding, any routine can become a battleground on which the child tests his control. A parent might say, "I dread to get up in the morning and face the thought of getting three meals into my child before bedtime!" For many children at this age, *nothing* about the meal will be right. They will object to any variation of a familiar food. I learned this lesson well when my niece screeched loud and long at my tofu sticks, which were a little shorter and narrower than those her mother made.

4 years   By four years, usually some of this rebelliousness has abated. Now more eager to be helpful and participate, the child is curious about all aspects of meal preparation. He may try to choose his own menu, he likes to serve himself at mealtimes, and he can talk without getting too distracted from eating. (A four-year-old has approximately 1550 words in his vocabulary!) Most children at four feel pretty good about themselves and may exhibit a pronounced interest in super heroes. K. Duncker (see bibliography) studied the effect of heroes upon food preference of preschoolers. The children were told a story in which the hero chose a sour food over a sweet one. Afterwards, the children showed a change in preference (temporarily, anyway) toward the food the hero liked.

Sweetness is now the most important factor determining food preference, with familiarity coming in second. Even at this early age, however, individual taste preferences begin to emerge. For example, my son liked raisins because they were sweet, but disliked dates, which were "too sweet."

5 years   The child is now adept at feeding himself and is social and talkative during meals. Parents will also notice much dawdling and wriggling. Food preferences are still strong, and the child will not easily accept casseroles or other mixed dishes.

School-Aged Children

When children enter school, they are inundated with cultural attitudes toward food. The biggest change that occurs in the body besides growth is replacing baby teeth with adult teeth. This change will not affect diet, except that during the short time he has loose front teeth, the child may be hesitant to bite down on apples or other crunchy foods.

Around age 7-8, children begin to show adult cultural attitudes toward food. A spaghetti and banana dish may be accepted at a younger age, but the school-aged child quickly learns that such a combination is strange. Under peer pressure a child may reject foods that seem unusual. Therefore, eating with other vegetarian families may provide a support for including certain types of food that will be branded as "strange" outside the child's immediate environment.

Studies of food likes and dislikes of children aged 6-9 have found that children like more foods than they dislike during these years. The average number of foods liked per child was 19.9 out of 25, with an average of 3 foods disliked. No significant sex differences in food preferences emerged except that boys liked a wider variety of foods than did girls. Unfortunately, this research included only one non-meat-eating child, and further research is necessary to determine whether vegetarian children might have a broader range of food likes due to the wider variety of foods offered to them in their diet. One encouraging finding from the study is that children have a more positive attitude toward food than parents believe. Children may not in fact eat all the foods they say they like, but a positive *attitude* can help establish good lifelong eating habits.

Important to remember is that children vary tremendously in their food preferences. For example, in the study mentioned, one child liked all 25 foods presented, while another liked only 4. Both children were included in the calculation of the average of 19.9 foods liked. Such variability is considered normal among children, so if your child varies from the average, in this case, do not be alarmed.

If your child dislikes many foods, however, make sure you offer *enough* of the liked foods to meet the daily requirements, while continuing to offer less preferred foods on a regular basis. You might also make an effort *with* the child to search for new foods to be added to the "like" category. Make sure all new foods are healthy ones, and consider only healthy foods when determining a like/dislike list.

I've learned from my son to take likes and dislikes with a grain of salt. For a while he'll want to eat a particular food often, but then one day will suddenly declare he has had enough and now doesn't like the food at all! This reversal has happened with tomatoes, yoghurt, and macaroni and cheese. Usually omitting the food from the diet for two or three weeks, without making a fuss over his stance, will work wonders.

The school-aged child is ready to learn about many aspects of nutrition. In fact, children may find a good nutrition program in the schools exciting and will help to spread the word. My son's father has been doing research recently in irradiation treatments of vegetables. My son comes back from a visit with him and enjoys telling me what he has learned; I can tell he realizes he has learned something important which affects him directly. This awareness of issues outside the home relating to diet gives the introduction of nutritional information a larger cultural context. A good program in school, complemented by parents' guidance can teach children the relationships between social responsibility and nutrition.

Children As Individuals

Despite all the studies on dietary preferences and patterns in child development, the average results may not match the behavior that you see in your own child. Parents may have difficulty distinguishing between what is characteristic of a particular child and what is just testing or unreasonable behavior that could, in the long run, be harmful. They want to be sensitive to their children's individual needs without raising difficult children, but how is that balance achieved?

The reasons why a child might reject a certain food can be divided into two basic categories: physical and behavioral. The physical response is a natural one. An infant will eat almost anything, but the stomach might reject the food and the baby will vomit. Toddlers will often taste foods, but spit them out if the taste is new; the food might be too bitter or too hot. In this case, the mouth and not the stomach has reacted negatively to the food. Older children and adults often reject a food before actually trying it because of its smell, color, or visual texture.

With the behavioral response, the child uses food to make an emotional statement. Typical behavioral eating disorders involve deviations from what we consider proper table manners: playing with food excessively, not using utensils properly, stuffing food into the mouth, complaining about food, refusing to feed oneself, or to sit at the table. Parents know that their children must eat well in order to grow and be healthy. When a child won't eat, the parent may naturally react with anxiety, unable to believe that picky eating or periods of refusing food will not result in ill health.

A young baby who refuses to eat is probably full or sick. One toddler might be on a food jag, while another might be rejecting a food because the body cannot tolerate it, as with an allergic response. A parent has to ascertain whether the child is using food refusal to express a feeling or if he is suffering a bad physical reaction. An emotional statement using food would necessitate a return to a level of acceptable table manners; for example, an older child who spits up food needs to be taught not to do so.

When a child is rejecting food or being a picky eater, the parent is better off addressing the underlying issue directly rather than through the medium of food. When mealtime becomes a battleground between parent and child, eating problems are likely to continue. Remaining calm and keeping in touch with our love and respect for the child becomes difficult if the family concentrates too much on a conflict over food. Instead of sharing the pleasures of food, the parent may try to trick the child into eating whatever is not wanted. The more this approach dominates eating, the more resentful both parent and child are likely to become. The following suggestions help parents steer a reasonable path between the need for a child to eat a healthy diet and the child's expression of food preferences:

1. Introduce a wide variety of foods. Since familiarity is a major factor in food preference, offering variety will increase the number of different kinds of food a child will actually eat. Even vegetarians sometimes have limited diets, eating primarily from a finite list of ingredients. Increasing the number of different grains, vegetables, legumes, seeds and nuts that your whole family eats not only assures better nutrition, but increases the likelihood that your child will continue to be a "good eater" as he grows.

When your child is between the ages of ten months and three years, you will encounter the least resistance to new foods, but don't give up introducing new foods if your child is older. Offer the new food in conjunction with a familiar one. A tiny taste or even smell of a new food, perhaps for several mealtimes, is often a more successful introduction to it than more heavy-handed exposure. Acceptance of some new foods cannot be achieved by offering them often within a short period of time. If a food has a very different flavor, texture, or visual appeal, acceptance may take time. Offer a new food on a regular basis, but don't always expect a quick and easy response.

2. *Don't force your child to eat more than a taste of anything.* There is nothing like parental pressure to make a child form a strong dislike of a food. Sometimes, when I suspect my son won't like a new food, I insist that he try it, but explain that even if he doesn't like it now, he might like it when he's older, because tastes change. In that way, neither he nor I label him as disliking a particular food forever. I strongly believe that having a child taste everything is important—with the exception of spicy hot foods.

3. *Offer small portions* and allow your child to have seconds. Too *much* food can discourage eating.

4. *Avoid using food as a reward.* When food is a reward for certain behavior, or dessert a reward for eating dinner, the emphasis on food as a healthy part of living shifts, leaving food in a secondary role. If dinner does not include a separate dessert, the child should be allowed to stop eating when he is full; if dessert is included, it should be healthy in its own right. When snacks are not available too near mealtime, the child's own appetite can determine how much to eat. It may seem risky, but if parents learn to trust their children's bodies, children learn to listen to their own real needs.

5. *Turn peer pressure to advantage.* As a child grows older, peer pressure becomes a factor in his appetite for certain foods and can sometimes be used to affect his diet positively. Discover healthy foods your child's peers eat and serve those. Invite his friends over and have them choose a menu from a preselected group of foods. Choose favorite foods of other vegetarian children who are friends of your child. I found that my son suddenly liked several new foods when he found out that another boy (one year older) liked them.

6. *Include your child in meal preparation.* Young children often enjoy being involved in the tasks they see their parents do every day. A child may choose a centerpiece for the table, make place mats, mix a salad, or do any small job that your time and patience and your child's abilities allow. Not only can this be a special time for you with your child, but you can pass along nutrition information in a natural way as you discuss the foods you are using. I find it more effective to discuss food when my son and I are getting dinner ready than to bring it up negatively ("You ate *what* for lunch at Timmy's?") or to make it dinner conversation ("Mom, that's boring").

7. *Don't become preoccupied with picky eating habits.* Reduce snacks, serve smaller portions at meals, invite people—especially other children—for a meal, and take the focus away from food. Your child will eat when he is hungry. You might also watch him for several days to see if at certain times the child does appear to be hungrier, and offer healthy mealtime foods in small portions at that time. (Do not provide desserts or junk foods at these times.) Possibly your child's body rhythms are different than yours; by starting from the times he is actually hungry and moving slowly towards the family mealtime, you may be able to change a "non-eater's" eating style. Bear in mind, too, that children who are growing quickly eat more than children who have reached a growth plateau. *What* a child eats is far more important than *how much* is eaten. But if your child also seems lethargic, see a doctor to make sure no factors of which you are not aware are affecting his appetite.

8. *Bear in mind that hunger and fatigue can affect a child's mealtime behavior.* As strange as it may seem, if a child is

too hungry, he may be unable to eat. Most preschoolers need food at least every four hours during the day, if not more often, and will actually lose their appetite if this need is not satisfied. Perhaps this response is a survival mechanism ensuring that hunger does not become too unbearable. Each child is different, of course, so watching your child's natural hunger cycles for a few days should help you determine how often food is necessary. There will probably always be a tension between when it is practical for you to prepare food and when your child wants to eat. The important thing to remember is that a loss of appetite can be a physical response to being over-hungry, comparable to a very tired child having trouble going to sleep.

Fatigue may also affect appetite. If a child is exhausted, the need for rest takes priority over appetite, which is one reason why a time of quiet activity right before lunch is often a part of a preschool program.

9. Watch what your child eats. Keep track of favorite foods, always remembering that tastes change. My son, who for two years loved carrots dipped in a smidgen of molasses, suddenly decided he liked carrots plain. He just as suddenly told me he preferred broccoli cooked. He keeps me aware of his changing tastes, and I try to assure that he gets those foods he likes. Keeping track of what your child actually does eat, may show you that his diet is healthier than you had thought.

10. Remember that young children usually prefer unmixed foods. If you give your child rice, a vegetable, tofu cooked lightly in nutritional yeast, and some fruit on a plate with none of the different foods touching, he will love it, but if you mix them into a casserole, you may not get much response. I find that offering a variety of different foods in small amounts assures that my son will clean his plate.

11. Remember that socially determined habits may not work for all people. Eating three meals a day is one example; young children often need to eat more frequently, which is why, in addition to the regular meals, snacks are provided twice a day in day-care centers. Along the same line, remember that a cold meal can be just as wholesome as a hot meal. (In fact, cooking food often *reduces* nutritional value.) Sandwiches are a favorite among children and can be made with a wide variety of ingredients to provide a healthy meal.

12. Remember that everyone has food likes and dislikes. Most children do not like as many foods as adults do. While in some instances a particular dislike may be emotionally based, in others the child honestly finds a food unpleasant in texture or flavor. Because children have more active taste buds than adults, some foods, such as romaine lettuce, may taste bitter to them. Children rarely enjoy spicy food. A common complaint from vegetarians is that children do not like beans. Fortunately, no one food is crucial for every child to eat. And making *some* allowances for individual preferences may show your child you respect his ability to make choices. Try substituting a food that will supply similar nutrients.

Eating Is A Family Ritual

Meals, particularly dinner, provide an opportunity for the whole family to get together. At this time family values and structure are strengthened. How a family eats and what a family eats are messages from the parents to the children about what is important. These values may be very different from house to house, depending upon the cultural background of each parent, which parent is dominant, and what values each has learned from the society in which she or he has been raised.

Here are some questions to help you look at the way your family treats food, and the messages you may be giving about your vegetarian diet (They pertain mostly to the dinner meal since breakfast is sometimes rushed and many families do not eat lunch together.):

Who decides what you eat? Whose preferences are taken most into account when planning a meal? Who shops for the food? Who prepares the meals? Who serves the meals and who cleans up?

These questions address the roles assumed by family members. Often the mother is primarily responsible for food preparation, shopping, and meal planning, but many meals

Table Manners

Good table manners are essential to a pleasant mealtime, but many parents may not know what behavior they can reasonably expect from their children. Parents may also not want to teach their children the same kind of formality at the table that they learned when growing up. Good table manners can show respect for the food as well as the other people sharing the meal. The following is a list of common table manners. You may find that they are too basic, or too strict. You might enjoy getting other ideas from your children!

- *Sit up straight at the table.* When a child slouches, it not only looks as if he doesn't care about his body, but also causes more food to be dropped on the floor, the chair, and the child's clothes, creating more clean-up work after the meal.

- *Eat slowly and chew your food well.* Chewing is the first step in proper digestion. Food breaks down as it mixes with saliva, allowing the body to assimilate it more easily.

- *Eat quietly and speak only when your mouth is empty.* There are, of course, exceptions to this rule, but the overriding principle is that no one likes to see partially chewed food in, or falling out of someone's open mouth. Gulping, slurping, and other loud noises are more common in some cultures than in others, but are usually associated with expressions of pleasure in eating. In our culture, such reactions to food are not acceptable. Also, it is difficult to understand someone when he talks with a full mouth.

- *Don't complain or whine about the food.* It's easy for children to get into the habit of finding fault with their food. Some parents tell them to try a little of everything on their plates. Other parents insist that they eat all the food on their plates. Whatever your position on the issue, helping children to find at least one positive thing about the food is more likely to result in a pleasant mealtime than adopting a negative stance.

are planned around the food preferences of the father. This kind of role stereotyping gives clear messages to children; it can discourage boys from active participation in meal preparation, for example. Children should see their fathers as well as their mothers interested and involved in a vegetarian lifestyle. The role that children themselves play in deciding what foods to eat is also very important. Allowing children to decide what the family will have for dinner one night a week (with parental guidance, if necessary, so that the meal is a healthful one) will make them aware of, and responsible for, the food they eat. It is also a direct way of informing them about what foods make up a nutritional meal.

Does your family eat together at dinner time? Is there a ritual to starting a meal?

Saying grace, holding hands, or having a moment of silence are examples of rituals that some families adopt, although such rituals may be rejected as artificial by adults who were forced into them as children. Whatever the form of the ritual, even the simple one of waiting until each person is seated, a family usually develops some signal to indicate that the meal may begin.

Is there a particular order to eating foods or is everything available at once? What other kinds of eating rules apply (taste everything, eat everything on your plate, no bread until you have finished your other food, etc.)?

These rules indicate to some extent the status that you put on different foods. You may know your child prefers some foods and so use those foods to encourage (bribe?) him into eating the less preferred foods. I usually give my son salad, fruits, breads, and main dish all at once, making sure that I know he can eat everything, but letting him decide what he eats first. He usually eats everything, but in a set order: fruit, bread, salad, main dish. I try to give him a little less food than will fill him up, so that when he finishes everything, he can choose seconds as he likes. This procedure provides him with some reason for finishing his food. It also removes my judgement of which foods are more or less desirable. Since everything I serve is good for him, I prefer not to emphasize some foods over others.

Do you have salt, pepper or other seasonings available on the table? To what extent can your children serve themselves, choose their own foods, season their own foods?

Naturally, parents' answers to these questions will change as their children grow older and are more knowledgeable about their own nutritional needs. When my son was five years old I still decided how much of each food he would eat. I thought he couldn't yet decide that for himself; even at my age, my eyes are bigger than my stomach at times. However, letting him choose what he would eat after he had finished his first serving allowed him some autonomy, which is very important in teaching a child awareness of food. Having children help in meal preparation and menu planning seems wiser at this age than letting them serve themselves. All children are different, and some may be ready to serve themselves in a knowledgeable way. At my son's day care, such choices are encouraged, and I know the children enjoy serving themselves. Again, if all the foods are healthy, this will be a safe practice.

What do you do during dinner? Who decides what you do, what you talk about? What is the eating atmosphere like?

The atmosphere at a meal is as important as what is served. Food is eaten in greater quantity and digested more efficiently if the mood is calm and happy. Tension hinders food consumption and interferes with digestion. Fighting at mealtime, especially about food, creates a bad feeling about the process of eating and even about the food itself. Such hostility runs counter to messages parents might consciously want to give their children about vegetarian food.

What manners do you insist upon at mealtime (such as not talking with a full mouth, staying seated until dinner is finished, sitting up straight, asking for food to be passed)? How long does a mealtime usually last? How do family members know that dinner is over?

The structure of a mealtime varies among households, but each family usually has a set of spoken and unspoken rules of behavior. There is a line between good table manners and a stiff atmosphere, just as there is a line that permissive parents need to draw to prevent unnecessary sloppiness. Table manners exist both to make people pleasant eating companions and to create a certain consciousness about the eating process. If you are eating, then your attention should be on eating. Food should be chewed well, not gulped down or lost in wild behavior. Firm and recognized simple rules will help a mealtime be more pleasant for everyone. If these rules are too strict, parents will find themselves nagging throughout the meal, which is counter-productive. A gentle reminder is often necessary, however, and need not spoil the occasion.

Some children are rowdy and have trouble being well-behaved at the table. A quiet time preceding dinner may help. Sometimes parents may have to require the child to eat alone rather than be too disruptive. This condition should not become a pattern, however, since its continuation would destroy the value of eating as a social event and a time for the whole family to be together.

Rituals can be empty or they can be meaningful. They always exist within a social structure, providing the backbone of security and strength. The evening family meal can be a time for family closeness and unity. Beyond providing good food, a meal brings together people who care about each other to share in an essential act of living.

UNDER PRESSURE 2

Whether we are overthrowing tradition or accepting it, we are all part of society. Our freedom of choice exists only with-in a complex and often unconscious set of social expectations and dynamics. Societal pressures *will* affect your child; you cannot prevent that. You may shield her from the direct influences of television, or of other families whose values are strikingly different from your own; you may try to structure and direct her social experiences in an attempt to reduce the effects of peer pressure, media, and big business agenda. But somehow, Transformers, Superman, and even "M—that's the letter for McDonald's!" seep in. Information comes from even the most casual contacts. Rather than withhold information from a child, one should help her learn how to evaluate it.

Certain challenges face the vegetarian family in a culture that does not support a healthy vegetarian lifestyle. In this chapter we will look at a variety of approaches to (1) the pitfalls in changing the family diet, (2) peer pressure, (3) celebrating holidays outside your own home, and (4) the temptations of junk food.

Vegetarian Families In Transition

"My husband and I have three children: Deena (7), Daniel (5), and Adam (2½). When we were first married, we ate the typical fast food diet. Luckily we had a healthy baby in spite of this, although she only weighed 6 lbs., 10 oz. Deena was raised on this same junk food diet and of course acquired a taste for such foods. We didn't begin changing our diet until after Daniel was born (I had a tiring and uncomfortable pregnancy with him, with morning sickness—I guess my body was pretty deprived of proper nutrition by then). We changed our diet very slowly—trying to exclude the obviously horrible stuff like cookies, ice cream, and sugar first. Then when Daniel was a year old, I read the *Supermarket Handbook* by the Goldbecks and had a major day of cupboard cleaning. We also decided to exclude red meats and eat only home-grown chicken and fish. We eat mostly vegetarian meals now, no sugar, only whole foods.

"We're concerned about our daughter. Since she ate junk food for so many years, it wiped out her taste for good wholesome foods. She is a very picky eater, which is difficult for us. We thought our older son was going to be the same way, but we discovered he was just imitating her bad habits and is slowly outgrowing that tendency. Our youngest is a great eater so far. The way you feed them from the beginning makes an obvious difference.

"However, I won't give up hope for our daughter to change eventually. Since we like harmony at mealtimes, we try to remain as loose as possible about her eating habits. In the mornings she will eat only a cereal made of whole wheat flakes with flaxseed. For lunch she will eat only peanut butter and honey sandwiches. For dinner she would be elated if we would allow her to eat either a tuna casserole or a grilled cheese sandwich. She will occasionally eat half of a raw carrot. She will not eat any other vegetable or fruit, but will drink

Some Definitions for the New Vegetarian

What kind of vegetarian are you? Everyone wants a label, so it is useful to know what these labels mean. You can choose what fits your lifestyle. Remember that not all diets are appropriate for all people at all times. When choosing your diet, consider your own children and your own individual needs, tastes, and temperaments.

A **Vegetarian** is someone who does not eat meat. The term refers to a broad category of vegetarians, including those people who avoid all meat except fish, as well as those who avoid only meat that came from the death of an animal and who might, therefore, eat dairy products and eggs.

A **Lacto-Ova-Vegetarian** is someone whose diet includes milk (lacto) and eggs (ova). This type of vegetarian diet is well-accepted and proven to be healthy for children.

A **Lacto-Vegetarian** is someone who includes milk and milk products in her diet but not eggs or foods that have eggs in them. This diet, while more conservative than the one above, is also a healthy diet for children.

A **Vegan** is someone who avoids milk, eggs, and all dairy products and by-products as well as all foods that contain these ingredients. The vegan diet is often lower in carbohydrates than the other vegetarian diets listed above. Parents must pay very careful attention to maintaining levels of caloric intake that are high enough for a child's proper growth and development on this diet. With adequate knowledge and supervision, this diet is healthy for children.

A **Fruitarian** is someone who eats only fruit and nuts, sometimes only fruit and nuts that have fallen naturally from the trees and bushes on which they grow. This diet is not appropriate for a child.

A **Macrobiotic** may or may not be a vegetarian. While the macro-biotic avoids meat and dairy products, fish and other seafood is an integral part of many macrobiotic diets. This diet is based on a highly developed and regimented philosophy of life taken from the Eastern principles of Yin and Yang. It is not recommended for children except those under the supervision of a very well-trained macrobiotic cook or doctor.

apple juice sometimes. The only grain she will eat is brown rice. That's about it! Not much of a varied diet. I give her a vegetarian chewable vitamin every day.

"I feel very concerned and frustrated at times about this. Do you know of any other parents in our predicament?"

Darla Karagianes, Sacramento, CA

Vegetarianism is new as a cultural movement in the United States; many families' diets and life styles are in transition. Children who are brought up to eat a vegetarian diet from the start often do eat better than children who switch over after eating a meat-centered diet with junk-food snacks. Parents may have difficulty seeing the trouble their children have readjusting. Important to remember is that the change to a vegetarian life style doesn't happen overnight; it is a process that may take years to complete.

Be prepared to allow time for vegetarianism to become a way of life, with ups and downs, even meat binges, as part of the process of changing. Eating meat during this transition time does not imply failure. Accept this setback, instead of dwelling on it: eat a healthy vegetarian meal next time! If the transition is slow, the result is likely to be more secure. Rushing things in a euphoria of new experience can actually be counter-productive. Once the euphoria wears off, the change may be harder to maintain. Not just a fad, vegetarianism is worth the time and effort it takes to convert a family's eating habits.

I have heard it said that children are led with ease but forced with difficulty. A child finds change especially difficult when it is not her own idea. Adults can be vegetarians for moral, religious, and economic reasons; a child won't necessarily understand these reasons right away. Involving your child in decision making and allowing her choices as you change your family diet will help her to be more comfortable with the process. While a young child may not be able to act upon an intellectual decision about what is good for her, she can feel strongly about a new philosophy when she is actively involved. Cleaning out the cupboards and planning menus together will encourage her to feel that this is a family project, not just something imposed from outside.

If the change to a vegetarian diet causes conflicts when your child eats with friends, it will be all the more important to make the transition fun, rather than fraught with resistance and disapproval.

You will help your child most by understanding your own beliefs so that you can be firm in them, knowing that the changes are not depriving her nutritionally. Having both parents firmly committed to the new diet will help. If one parent still eats meat and/or junk foods while the other disagrees, children may get confused; loyalty, rather than better health may become an issue. Keep in mind that white-sugar desserts are not an expression of love. The strongest statement of caring you can offer is a healthy vegetarian diet.

When parents live together, differences in dietary values usually occur. When parents live separately, chances are good that the differences will be even greater. For some divorced parents, the child's diet may become symbolic of the fears one parent has about the other's ability to take good care of the child. A vegetarian parent may run into resistance if unhealthy foods and meat are the staple of the non-vegetarian parent's home.

Transition Time: Making The Change
Changing Your Buying Habits

Before you change your eating habits to those of a vegetarian life style, you will have to change your buying habits. This can be done all at once with a house cleaning in which you and your children ceremoniously clear your kitchen of all the food that you plan to stop eating. Or, as foods run out, you can replace them with healthy alternatives. The chart below gives some suggestions for replacing old foods with new foods.

Old Foods	New Foods
Baked Goods—refined breads, store-bought cookies	rice cakes, whole grain breads and pastries
Drinks—sodas, sweetened juices	natural fruit juices with selzer water for fizz, homemade fruit and vegetable juices, nut milks
Proteins—meat and dairy products	grains, legumes, tofu
Sweeteners—white sugar, artificial sweeteners	apple juice, honey, rice syrup, maple syrup
Salt—table salt	miso, sea salt, sea vegetable powder, soy sauce, herbs and spices
Flours and Pastas— all processed (usually white) flours and pastas	whole wheat and other whole grain flour and pastas, vegetable pastas
Oils and Fats—butter, cream, mayonnaise	unrefined vegetable oils, nut butters/spreads, soy margarine

It may be difficult not to let basic issues such as food choices be an outlet for the tension of unresolved, unrelated differences between two separated parents. Seeing good nutrition undercut at the other house is frustrating. But since the other parent probably will not change, especially after divorce, downplaying the difference may be best. Concentrate on the food you serve in your own house, talk to your child about how you feel, but don't drag in the other parent's faults or even nutritional abuses. Children won't easily accept information presented as an accusation or even a downgrading of the other parent; indeed, such a strategy may backfire.

It is hard to draw the line between acceptance of other influences on your child and protection of her health. But outside influences are bound to come from many directions, and unless your child's health is endangered (in which case you may need support for your position from a doctor or representative from the medical world), my advice is simply to act with dignity. Don't use food in a personal fight with the other parent. Provide your child with a model: yourself. Respect your own choices, and you will pass your respect for vegetarianism on to your children. Compassion is part of vegetarianism, after all, and may be more crucial in the long run than the candy or hot dog your child gets from the other parent this weekend.

Change will be most effective if it begins with *you* and is spread with love and joy. Work with your family slowly, accepting any resistance as a natural part of the process. Serve food that tastes good, using familiar ingredients at first; listen to your family's tastes and responses; and refrain from setting up the transition in a context of good/bad or right/wrong, so that the greatest change may occur. As Paalo Airola says, a negative state of mind can undo all the good work that one is trying to achieve with vegetarian nutrition.

Peer Pressure

Choosing to be a vegetarian family may mean building a conflict into your child's life. She wants to belong to a mainstream peer group, but stands out as peculiar because of her diet. This difficult situation can in turn set up a conflict for the parent—"In this stress-filled world, do I want to add to my child's problems?" For many parents, the value of the vegetarian diet will far outweigh any temporary difficulty their children may have in fitting into a peer group. For the children, however, the conflict may feel severe. Parents need to be sensitive to this conflict and to offer support.

In the long history of people learning how to live together, we have developed rules of acceptable social behavior, which vary from culture to culture. Anarchy (the absence of such rules) seems to be only theoretical rather than practical. While some rules of social behavior become institutionalized into laws, most are much more informal. We usually do not learn to be nice to others simply because the Bible says so, but because the admonitions of our parents ring on in our ears.

Most children spend the majority of their waking hours with their parents and are extremely dependent upon them for survival. This dependence seems to make children particularly susceptible to their parents' values at an early age. With time, however, the length and number of separations from a child's parents increases, as does her exposure to the culture at large.

A peer group is the first socializing force outside the family. Within the peer group, a child practices skills of relating, learning sensitivity and awareness of other people, and cooperation. Discovering what it takes to get along with others is often confusing. The child learns patterns of relating to others from the family, but, according to Bossard and Boll in *Sociology of Child Development*, "however they [the patterns] work at home, the peer world renders its own verdict. . . .

In the course of this learning process, many a child comes to discover that there is a fundamental difference between the response patterns emphasized to him in the family world and those prescribed for him in the peer world...he must live in both worlds, and at a time when he lacks insight into the peculiarities of life, parents, and his peers."

A true sense of caring seems to develop from being cared about. A child finds pleasure in being thoughtful to someone else, and learns the fact that she is not going to have many friends if she is cruel and thoughtless to others. Small children quickly develop a sense of who the "good guys" and "bad guys" are, who the neighborhood bully is, and which kids are the most popular.

Being popular means being liked. It feels good to be liked, to be respected. While the desire to be popular may not be equally strong in all children, no one can deny the importance of the desire to be accepted. Children who feel themselves to be outsiders may develop other strengths, but fear of inadequacy is never a comfortable feeling.

Children nearly always become involved in a peer group; most experience a growing desire for social contact. Until about twenty years ago, experts believed and taught that children under age four or five primarily engaged in "parallel play" with each other. In other words, they played next to each other, but not with each other. The recent explosion of use of day care for young children in the United States can be at least partially credited for a change in this theory. Young children, even babies, are now observed to be very aware of one another, seeking each other out, often responding to other children before adults! It is easier to learn from someone whose size and experience are more comparable, who is more familiar with the "secret language of childhood."

How a child fits into a peer group is very important to the way she views herself. Although peer pressure may seem to be as oppressive and impersonal as any set of institutional rules, keep in mind that a peer group is made up of individual children. Some will be leaders, some will be followers—eagerly or reluctantly.

In the culture of childhood, "good" children are not necessarily the most popular children. Daring, initiative, creativity, and special skills such as good verbal or physical capabilities are often more important than the virtues parents might prefer, such as going to bed without fussing, abstaining from violence, being nice to others. Being popular means that a child is more likely to affect the values, preferences, and dynamics of the group. Popular children are usually those who have been particularly sensitive to the nuances of dominant adult behaviors and are socially aggressive themselves. Because of their simulation of adult social behaviors, they are more likely to spread adult cultural values. This phenomenon suggests two ideas for vegetarian parents: first, it makes sense to acquaint your children with influential adult role models whom you yourself admire, and second, a popular child can provide an access route to other children for a concerned parent or teacher who can then channel useful information through the child to all members of the peer group.

Do you see your child as a leader, a participant, or a victim in her peer group? How does she view herself? Think about yourself with your friends—are you a leader, follower, participant? Who makes decisions? Often, children are most comfortable with social roles learned from their parents. Are you satisfied with your social role? If not, you may be able to think of ways to change that might give your child more flexibility as well.

Your child may be fortunate to be involved with peers who do not think a vegetarian diet is strange. But peer pressure is often only a reflection of societal pressure, and in most societies, vegetarians are a minority and inevitably considered odd. Willingness to accept differences seems to be a major difficulty in childhood peer groups. This reluctance is not surprising, since most adults have the same difficulty in feeling comfortable with people who are perceived as very different. Can you think of someone you don't like because they seem ("are") so different than you are? Would you agree with the following statement by Mark Braunstein, who describes himself as a "radical vegetarian"?

"If animals are our friends, then carnivores are our enemies." Accepting other people means treading a fine line between appreciating them for who they are and being open to new ideas, while still standing up for one's own values. Sticking with our own familiar values is easier, even if it means giving up the challenge of variety.

This issue is complex enough for adults. Children are still defining themselves and in many cases do not have their own values established clearly enough to be sure they are right when their peers hold a different value. Parents can aid by listening: encourage your child to describe any areas of conflict, and talk about what it felt like when you were caught in a similar conflict, or how you handled such a situation. When a child is caught between pleasing her parents and pleasing her peer group, the only bridge is the development within the child of her own values, her own self-affirmation. This long process is complicated by the need to belong, to be accepted, to be part of a community. Parents do not need to dominate; they do need to be sensitive to this conflict and offer support.

Holidays

Food is often the center of traditional holiday celebrations. Since vegetarian families frequently spend holidays with their non-vegetarian relatives, a natural area of tension arises. Interviews with vegetarian parents in Ithaca, New York, show a variety of ways to approach this venture from one's own kitchen.

Some vegetarians avoid traditional blood family gatherings and create their own new families:

"The holidays that we celebrate in this country seem to be tied to certain food experiences, most of which don't fit into a vegetarian, whole-foods diet. For this and other reasons, I have pulled away from celebrating many of these holidays and have been drawn towards alternative celebrations. These are good opportunities for establishing new, healthier traditions. We don't have to overdose on any particular food, good or bad.

"If we do have food on a holiday, a potluck meal is important. Solstice celebrations are perfect occasions for the celebration of locally produced foods. The institution that I work for sponsors an annual vegetarian feast that involves a fairly fancy dinner for about 200 people. I think this kind of event legitimizes the vegetarian diet in the eyes of the children who take part."

Dan Hoffman, Ithaca, NY

Other vegetarians, more commonly, continue the contact with their families on holidays, but provide alternative foods for their children:

"When we go to my family's house or to a friend's house for holidays where I know they're probably going to be serving meat and a lot of sugary foods, I'll take something that I've made so that there's a variety of things to choose from. I'll tell Eli that he can have one of the junky things, but that if he's going to eat more, he has to choose from this other group of things that I have brought. It's usually up to him whether he has meat or not. We've spent a number of Christmases and Thanksgivings with people who have served meat and I can't remember one time that he chose to eat it."

Carol Bone, Ithaca, NY

Halloween is the biggest problem holiday for parents. The ritual of exploring the neighborhood at night with friends is exciting, but the adventure is often entirely centered around getting sweet things to eat. It is impossible to avoid; all children find out about the *treat* in trick-or-treat through school, stores, television, and friends.

Some parents resign themselves to Halloween, especially as their children get older:

"I figure Halloween is their business—they just orgy out for a couple of days, and then it's over. It doesn't seem to do any permanent harm. Halloween was so special to me as a kid that I'm not going to get on my high horse and spoil the whole thing for them. I've heard of parents who give their kids lists of houses they can go to where they'll be given healthy foods, but I think that's too much parental control and it ruins the fun of it."

Jane Palomountain, Ithaca, NY

"When Eli does get candy, we have a deal that he can have one piece every couple of days—he rations himself and doesn't ask for any more than that. It's hard to tell—I think it's possible to be too strict; I could be making such a big deal out of it that I'm missing what's important."

Carol Bone, Ithaca, NY

"When Halloween comes, it's a nightmare, but I don't prohibit her from eating candy. In fact, what happens is that she ends up rejecting a lot of the candy she gets. She just doesn't like it that much. I guess I'm lucky."

Judy Saul, Ithaca, NY

"At Halloween, I used to give only healthy treats like fruit and raisins, but lately Kristin has been complaining—maybe she's embarrassed. When she gets candy, she shares it with me and I like that, so I shouldn't be totally opposed to buying it myself, I guess."

Becky Logan, Ithaca, NY

Other parents draw stricter lines, feeling that the long range effects of healthy eating are more important than the fleeting Halloween pleasure:

"This year we forbade trick-or-treating. We started thinking and talking about it about a month ahead of time—we
said we probably wouldn't let them go, so we would like to
go out to dinner or go bowling instead. We wanted to get
away from the house, because it would be hard on them to
have other children knocking on the door. I didn't buy anything to give out, either. Halloween has lost its fun. It just
happened that some friends of ours invited us out for a potluck meal with vegetarian chili. We bobbed for apples and
had a lot of fun. We all drove into town in the back of an
oversized pick-up and it was a beautiful night. The kids didn't
complain at all. Maybe since they'd heard so often that they
couldn't go, they knew it was a lost cause. In any case, they
had fun doing something different."

Carol and Dan Peterson, Ithaca, NY

I took my son trick-or-treating for the first time when he
was two and a half. I tried the method mentioned above of
having my son go only to houses where it had been prear-
ranged that healthy foods would be given out. Fortunately,
I live in a neighborhood with a high percentage of vegetarians; there were about fifteen houses on the eight-block jour-
ney. It was quite exciting for us all, parents and kids, to be
outside together in the October evening. The children all got
their bags filled with:

homemade toffee
popcorn balls
fruit and nut bags
apples
homemade carob fudge, wrapped in foil
peanuts in the shell
pumpkin bread muffins
homemade cookies

One advantage of going to homes where you have prear-
ranged healthy food choices with people you know is that

home-baked goods can be given to the children. Most children who trick-or-treat treat randomly are not allowed to eat even the fruit they are given for fear of razor blades and poison that might be hidden in them. With the Tylenol poisoning scare that year, I was especially glad to know that my son would get food only from people I knew. The Halloween trek ended at a home which had been decorated as a spook house. Except for the unwieldy number of children and parents in one mass, I would certainly say that for young children (up to age six or seven) such an approach provides the pleasure and excitement of Halloween and eliminates junk food and candy intake. It does not reduce overall sugar intake, however: fudge, toffee, and cookies, no matter how healthy, provide a very heavy dose. However, I think all of us felt that the damage was slight, and the evening gave us a special sense of community.

Older children who want to go out on their own will not be as likely to go only to preselected houses, especially if they go with friends who come from families with different attitudes toward nutrition. Providing an alternative group celebration and thus removing the opportunity to trick-or-treat may be the only way to insure against a sudden overload of junk food. For many parents without this alternative celebration, a day or a week of candy may provide them with an opportunity to help their children discover what happens to their bodies when they consume a lot of sugar. The best way to make a difficult situation worthwhile is to learn as much as you can from it. If you have candy around, study what goes into candy, read to your children from *Sugar Blues* by William Dufty, have them chart their own behavior, suggest they practice self-control by regulating their own intake of sugar, and talk about how they feel.

"Jasmine has been a vegetarian all her life, all five years of it. She is strong, healthy, and bright. I often wondered what effect her vegetarianism would have on her socially, how her peer group would relate to her, and how she would relate to them about her vegetarian diet. The experience we have had so far has been very positive and uplifting. Her friends in the neighborhood have found our home to be the preferable place at mealtime, or snack time, really any time something is going on in the kitchen. Her friends eat the traditional American white bread and hot dog fare at home, but in the realms of our whole wheat spinach noodles with cashew gravy, or scrambled tofu breakfast, they are transformed into natural culinary experts. Our conversations often cover the subjects of health and nutrition, we all share our knowledge, the children always have a lot to share. And they have a remarkable ability to learn when the desire to learn is present. There is no pressure put on them to eat the new foods, we told them they may eat only what they wanted. However, we did ask them not to criticize the things they didn't care for so as not to negatively influence the others. With open minds and hungry bellies, they dug into these unrecognizable delights with the curiosity that only children seem to have in such abundance. The kids liked most of what they tried, some things were only so-so, but it seemed like if I just explained to them how highly nutritional the foods were, they would try them again, approaching it with that idea in mind. One such example of that is when I served a heaping mound of alfalfa sprouts in the middle of a relish tray. Everything got eaten except the sprouts, we talked about them a little, then everyone tried them again. Soon they were asking for more.

"Our fruit salad extravaganzas are one of our favorite meals to make together. It really happens fast with so many little hands scooping, chopping, peeling. We all have so much fun working together, seeing all our efforts make a beautiful rainbow of colors, shapes and sizes. This particular dish has even been added to some of the other families' menus. The kids went home and taught their moms how to make a simple, fresh fruit salad. We are all growing so much from this opportunity to learn abut ourselves and what we need. Jasmine likes to know why things are healthy or not, what vitamins are, and which foods contain which vitamins. One day I began reading to her from a nutrition list of various foods and their vitamin content. She insisted I read the entire chart to her. Much of the information she has retained, and I am very proud of her when she chooses the strawberries for her treat because, as she informs me, they are so high in vitamin C and so fresh and delicious.

"It is important that vegetarian children be well informed. They must have accurate information. It is not enough to say, 'White bread is no good for you.' Children must understand what refining is, so they can realize that junk food isn't poison, or that it won't make them sick to eat dinner at their friend's house, but rather, for optimum health and growth, every individual has the right to make a choice about what to eat. Correct eating patterns can reflect a lot about a person's total well-being. Children understand this simple harmony between nature and health. Natural foods make more sense to a child's inquisitive mind and every child has the right to know about the foods they consume. One day when I asked one of Jasmine's friends if she wanted soy milk or cow's milk, she looked at me as if I were mad. She said she wanted regular milk, so I showed her the two cartons and explained that what she called regular milk was the cow's milk. She gasped, 'Ugh! I'll never drink milk again!' I hadn't the heart to tell her where Big Macs come from.

"Life is full of exciting adventures, and raising a vegetarian child is one of the most fulfilling. Perhaps the most important thing we've learned is to accept others regardless of their diet, to respect every individual's freedom of choice, and to illustrate daily the close connection with our bodies that proper eating patterns develop. Some of Jasmine's friends have said they would like to become vegetarians when they grow up. Whether they do or not, I'm sure the experiences we've had together will influence them and their families in a number of ways in the years to come."

Debbie Elias, Kalamazoo, MI

Junk Foods and Snacking

"Meat doesn't have sugar in it, right Mom?"—Nikolas, age three.

Snacking brings to mind sugar, junk foods, and obesity. I notice my son often wants something to eat when he's bored, or perhaps that's when he notices his hunger most clearly. For adults, snacking is often a habit, relieving stress or boredom. We snack absent-mindedly or compulsively; I have friends who cannot keep any snack foods in the house because they will eat them immediately, stuffing themselves beyond the point of pleasure.

For children, however, snacking may be necessary. Most children consume about 1/3 of their calories in snacks. With a high-energy output, their bodies may not be able to take in enough nutrition at mealtimes to last the hours until the next meal. Day-care centers invariably give mid-morning and afternoon snacks, usually involving children in the preparation.

Snacks should really be considered mini-meals, rather than a bad habit for children to grow out of. In a good article on "Children and Junk Food" by Annemarie Colbin (*East-West Journal*, Sept. 1982, pp. 52-57), one mother says that she views lunches as snacks and makes breakfast at home a substantial meal, assuring a nutritious start for an active day. This meal is complemented by snack foods readily eaten by her children for lunch. Making breakfast into a mealtime that includes vegetables and grains is most successful if the whole family takes part. I find that my son is starving in the mornings and rarely is hungry at lunchtime, so such an idea makes great practical sense to me.

It is easy to think of nutritious snacks, and usually easy to get children to eat them if nothing else is available. However, as children begin to visit friends, watch television advertising, and recognize supermarket goodies at the checkout counters, they discover a whole world of sweet junk foods out there. Parents cope with these outside influences in a variety of ways:

"Sean hasn't been exposed too much to other kids' eating habits, so I don't believe that he realizes yet that he eats differently than they do. If he is with friends who are eating something like oreos, I try to provide an alternative. And believe it or not, the kids will often prefer what he's got. I make our baked goods, including small doses of candy, so I can control exactly what he gets. I use honey, molasses, or barley malt as sweeteners. Instead of Kool-aid or soft drinks, he gets apple juice and tea. I use bulk tea, forming my own blends. Recently I made apple leather for my kids. It was a lot simpler than I imagined and ten times as delicious, and a good way to use up the old apples left over from last year's crop."

Terresa McConville, Snowflake, AZ

"I have some concerns about being a vegetarian in a world of meat-eating, junk-food junkies. It's becoming difficult to deal with relatives, even though they know where we stand. They're always saying things to Dyani like, 'Don't you want a hamburger or a nice sugary cookie?' They think it's a big joke. Her cousin offers her junk food, but so far Dyani has been turning it down. Pretty soon, though, I know she will be wondering why their food is 'bad.' She can't see long- or even short-term effects from a bad diet. To make things more difficult, we are vegans. We eat soy ice cream, and when Dyani sees kids eating cow's milk ice cream, she thinks it's the same thing. How do you explain to a two year old that cow's milk isn't good for you when she sees everyone else drinking and eating it?"

Lilia Bathceller, Bayport, NY

"Jamie has grown up with only good nutritional snacks available to him, so there have been times when he hasn't even recognized cake or candy! He is used to the kind I make—applesauce, carob, carrot or spice cakes without frosting. This Christmas he refused a candy cane from Santa, much to my delight. At age one and a half he played with two rolls of candy that someone had pushed into his hands before I could say no. He never even opened them, he just liked the pretty colors."

Katie Day-Schirmer, Hesperia, MI

The packaging of junk foods is often as persuasive as the taste. Many health food companies are now sprucing up their packaging in order to compete in the marketplace. Pretty colors and shiny wrappers appeal to children. Once my son desperately wanted a brand of peanut butter only because there was a picture of Superman on the jar's label. For some perverse reason, I broke down and bought the brand for him, only to discover he really did not like the taste as much as the kind we usually have. Upon a suggestion from a friend, I kept the jar and filled it with our regular peanut butter. I felt odd giving in to the packaging, but my son realized that it *was* the picture on the jar rather than the contents that he had wanted, so it became a good lesson for us both.

"When Stacy was born, I was determined to keep sugar out of her diet. When we are out, I tell her that she can't have certain foods because of sugar content. I had wondered if it would ever cause a problem by making her feel left out. My answer came one day at a La Leche League meeting. Everyone was standing around the refreshments, so Stacy went up and asked, 'Does this have sugar in it?' When the reply was 'No,' Stacy said, 'Well, good, then I can eat it.' Not too many three-year-olds are concerned with diet and health. I was so glad I had stuck to my instincts."

Becky Glasburn, Thousand Oaks, CA

"We live in a tiny community (twenty-five people) where I can have a lot of control over my son's exposure to candy and sweets, and I let my feelings be known to the other three or four mothers in town. I guess the best defense is to live away from the sugar life style. Beyond that, all you can do is to lay a foundation and let your relatives and friends know how you feel. I've had to tell Grandma not to offer sweets. I feel like a hawk, but it's important to me, since I'm the one who has to deal with a buzzed-out child. Be firm with all concerned!"

Debi Corcoran, Essex, MT

"When our son was five, his mother and I were very strict about avoiding junk food. We didn't provide him with any candy or sugary things and tried to develop in him enough self-discipline so that he would avoid these things himself. That was successful up until he was six or seven. Then peer pressure, older relatives, everything combined to break down his willingness or ability to resist those kinds of foods. I don't want to put too much pressure on him, knowing that he has to exist in both of these worlds. I think the most I can do for him at this point is to set an example for him, and to expose him to other situations that encourage vegetarianism and natural foods."

Dan Hoffman, Ithaca, NY

"I don't preach about it very much, but I repeat the basic message that if they want to be healthy and good looking, (which they do care about at ages nine and eleven), then they have to eat well. I buy what I consider good food, so most of the time they have no choice. They do have money, but fortunately my boys are so addicted to video games that playing Pac Man is far more important than buying a Mars bar.

"I think that the more strenuously you try to forbid something, the more desirable you make it. If you let them have orgies now and then, it won't be so desirable. If they get to watch television and eat junk food at my parents' house, they don't care about it as much when they are with me.

"My younger boy, who is a little more self-aware, has said that when he eats candy and sugar, he doesn't like the way it makes him feel. He still does it sometimes anyway, but he knows what will happen. It affects his behavior: he gets spacey and says he feels scattered. My older boy may be hyperactive. He gets more aggressive when he eats sugar, and starts being a crybaby. I'll say, 'Why are you crying like that?' and he'll say he's always like that when he eats candy."

Jane Palomountain, Ithaca, NY

"Alice really likes breakfast cereals, so I compromise by getting Grapenuts and spoon-sized shredded wheat. The Grapenuts seem pretty clean, and shredded wheat has BHT or BHA in it, but no sugar or color additives. We don't have a television, and until about two months ago she had never watched television. She has started going to a neighbor's house and I've noticed that in the last two months of watching television she's become more attracted to eating breakfast cereals. She knows their names from the cartoon ads, so she says to me, 'How about Fruit Loops?' or 'Do you know they make a cereal just like doughnuts?' I've always talked to her a lot about why I do what I do, so I've explained to her that these foods have lots of chemicals and sugar. She came home one day, quoting the Wonder Bread commercial, something about how it doesn't have to be whole-wheat to be healthy. She's quick; she always picks these things up. So I explained to her that they take all the nutrients out of commercial white bread and put in chemicals, substitutes for the nutrients, which I don't think are as good."

Judy Saul, Ithaca, NY

Sometimes parents feel as if they are depriving their children of a normal experience by not feeding them candy and other junk foods. Parents would like their children to be happy. It is difficult to make your child refuse candy when her face lights up at the offer. I remember vividly a day when I came home from third grade to find that for the first time ever my mother had baked cookies with red sugar sprinkles for Valentine's Day. Since we rarely even had dessert with meals, this treat was unheard of, and I was filled with gratitude that my mother loved us enough to do this forbidden thing. At the same time, I respected her for feeding us so well.

Children learn a lot by example. This mirroring may be hard for vegetarians who have never been able to break their own bad snacking habits. It is ineffective to ask a child to exercise restraint if you give in yourself, because the double message cannot be resolved. Plenty of forces outside the home set up conflicts for a child trying to figure out right and wrong. If you want your children to exclude junk and empty calorie foods from their diet, then you must set the example. I am cautiously optimistic that with a consistent message in the home, more and more schools beginning to educate children in nutritional awareness, and the indirect support of the growing number of healthy vegetarians throughout society, children will probably get the message.

One of the major problems caused by junk food is the conflict it often creates between parents and children. Supermarkets keep their candy by the check-out counter; the sweeter cereals, especially those advertised most heavily on television, are put on the lower shelves, in plain view and reach of even the youngest children who walk by.

Parents can have more influence in the community than we often imagine, however. In 1985, the *New York Times* reported a wonderful story of cooperation between a consumer and responsive marketers. In response to a complaint from Margaret Halpin, a concerned parent, Kroger supermarkets in Cincinnati and St. Louis established a candy-free checkout line in each store. A giant sign above the register reads "Mom! This is a No Candy checkout line. It's here to make your shopping trip more pleasant." Kroger officials have said they are pleased with the experiment. You may want to suggest this plan to the manager of your own local grocery.

Nevertheless, I have found that my son's excitement about these products is to some extent unavoidable. With great delight at age three, he would run up to the candy and cookie shelves in a small corner store and yell, "Mommy, look at these yukkies!" He was just as excited as if he'd called them "candy and cookies," but by referring to the foods with a derogatory name, giving heed to the adult disapproval he expected, he could still express his excitement.

For his birthday one year, my son received a board game called "Candyland," in which the players pick cards and move along a path through "Peppermint Forest," "Gingerbread Plum Tree," "Gumdrop Mountains," "Lollipop Woods," and "Molasses Swamp" to the final goal of the "Gingerbread House." Six cards, each picturing a different kind of sweet food, are picked to move the players rapidly along the course. I had very mixed feelings about the game, with its obvious indulgence in candy fantasies. My son wanted to play the game as often as possible. He took the special cards with sweets pictured on them to bed, pretended to eat them. He got tremendous delight from them, and I watched carefully to see if there would be any cross-over to real food. There wasn't any, to my surprise. He never asked for any of the items, never, in fact, treated them as anything but fantasy materials. Within a few months, he got tired of the game and we put it away.

Once children are in school and on their own, sometimes with their own money to spend, parents have considerably less control. Continuing to provide healthy and delicious food at home, to educate children, and to be firm in one's own personal commitment to healthy living will go a long way. Offering tasty and healthy snack alternatives in social settings will not only reassure your child that eating well does not mean a spartan diet, but will also educate and encourage other children to join in. Some children can learn to monitor their own behavior in response to large doses of sugar, but other children do not have a recognizable body reaction and will have a harder time understanding that this food is not good for them.

Curiosity and responsiveness to television and peer advertising are normal. When I am at the supermarket check-out counter with my son, he is fascinated by the candy and gum display as we wait. He asks me the name of each sweet, and wants to sort the ones that are in the wrong boxes. I tell him the names and allow him to sort them. He seems to understand implicitly that he cannot have any, and doesn't ask. I notice that satisfying his curiosity on an intellectual level seems to reduce his anxiety about, and desire for, eating them. I often see children trying to sneak candy when their parents tell them not to touch or to stay away. Children *are* curious; given information along with a consistent, firm message that these foods are bad for health, they don't appear to be harmed by this curiosity. I think, in fact, my son is learning and practicing his own self-restraint, which in the long run will be much more effective than any outside control.

Fast Foods for Busy Vegetarian Parents

Most vegetarians shrink from the idea of "fast foods". The term suggests food that is barely edible—too much salt, too few nutrients, too high in empty carbohydrates, sugars, and harmful preservatives. Working vegetarian parents who find themselves short on time may wish there were healthy fast foods, no matter how contradictory that phrase might sound. It is a testament to the number of vegetarian parents that there is now a response to this growing consumer demand. A well-stocked health food store offers several items made from natural ingredients suitable for fast preparation. For example, the following items are available at my local health food store.

Tofu burger mix—add tofu and fry. Ingredients are toasted brown rice flour, corn meal, powdered soy sauce, dehydrated vegetables, nutritional yeast, toasted sesame seeds, arrowroot flour, miso powder, and spices.

Frozen okara patties—bake for 12-15 minutes. Ingredients are textured soy protein concentrate, wheat gluten, egg whites, okara (cooked soy pulp), soybean oil, potatoes, yeast extract, skim milk, onion, sea salt, carrageenan (a natural seaweed extract), vegetable gum, spices, paprika, oil of celery, and turmeric.

Mochi flat cakes—bake for 10 minutes. Ingredients are sweet brown rice, water, sesame seeds, garlic, onion, arame (seaweed), soy sauce, and tapioca powder. Mochi flat cakes can be eaten as muffins, in a casserole, or used as the base for an open sandwich. Sweet brown rice contains more protein and is more easily digested than other brown rices.

Macaroni and cheese—ingredients are pasta (semolina and Jerusalem artichoke flour) and cheese (corn flour, cheddar cheese, buttermilk, and natural cheese flavor).

Quick cooking wholegrain barley—takes 10-12 minutes to cook in boiling water. Good as a dinner grain, pilaf, or in soups.

Sesame burger mix—mix, let sit for 15 minutes, bake or fry. Ingredients are sesame meal, soya granules, raw wheat germ, natural soya powder, dried miso, nutritional yeast, dehydrated onion and parsley, garlic powder, and spices.

Whole grain and sesame cereal—available in both a pilaf texture and a puffed cereal mixture. Ingredients are slightly hulled whole oats, long grain brown rice, rye, hard red winter wheat, triticale, raw buckwheat, barley, and dehulled sesame seeds.

In addition to the above mentioned items, there are now healthy canned goods such as soups and sauces which are made without salt, sugar and preservatives. Walnut Acres, a well-stocked health food mail order store, is a great source for such foods. It was the sole source for my mother's purchases when she brought whole grains and other natural foods to our home when I was young.

There are a variety of pasta forms—spaghetti, shells, rigatoni, fettucini, lasagne, macaroni—now made from whole flours, spinach, artichoke, and other vegetable powders, rather than the less nutritious white, processed flours. There are nut butters from many kinds of nuts, a wide variety of cheeses made without rennet, and an even wider variety of healthy breads, crackers, chips, and snack foods available. All of these are a help to the busy parent who is unable or reluctant to spend a large amount of time preparing meals.

Of course, there is a cost to any prepackaged food. The price of the food is higher and some nutrient value is lost in the processing, even though this loss may often be minimal. Balancing healthy meals with a very busy life is a situation that each parent must face.

At the very least, these new foods offer an alternative for unusually busy parents and reduce any temptation to let the child eat foods that have little or no nutritional value. One of the bigger concerns of starting a vegetarian diet seems to be that it will take too much time to prepare healthy meals. These "fast" foods will help new vegetarian parents make some meal preparations faster and will, therefore, increase the chance of a successful transition to a healthier diet.

Another feature of many of these foods is that, as your children grow increasingly capable (not to mention independent), they will be able to make healthy meals for themselves. Children take pride in preparing foods. If they know how to make nutritious meals that don't require a lot of preparation time, they are assured of healthier diets as teenagers and young adults.

But don't get stuck in a routine of preparing only convenience health foods. Even the busiest parents should try to find time to make a meal "from scratch," both for nutritional reasons and because children need to learn that food has an original form that is neither prepackaged nor "fast." When choosing prepackaged vegetarian foods, use the following guidelines to obtain the highest quality in what you buy.

- Look for locally produced foods first. The ingredients are more likely to be fresher, which usually means a higher nutritional value.

- Read the list of ingredients. Salt is often included (usually in parentheses) even though the package says "All Natural" or "No additives." Sugar may be included on a package that proclaims "No Salt," directing your attention to the one asset it may have.

- When considering a food, look at the level of processing involved. Each step of processing removes you from the original food. In many cases, especially when food is produced locally, the difference may be slight. But beware of foods that look too fancy: money that was spent on marketing and packaging would have better been spent on making the product more wholesome. Overpackaging is also ecologically irresponsible, another clue to the attitude of the manufacturer.

- Get recommendations from other shoppers at a health-food store, other parents, children, and store workers. Many health-food stores send out flyers or newsletters and might be willing to include information that would be useful to you as a parent.

(Note: To the new vegetarian palate, some "health" foods may seem tasteless and therefore unattractive. Part of this may be due to a cynical tongue and can be overcome with time and a little spice. But a positive recommendation from a respected peer can do wonders for a child's openness to a new food.)

Mail-Order Foods

Because there are many vegetarian parents who do not have natural foods grocery stores nearby, it is essential to be able to shop by mail. Naturally, this list of mail-order food sources is incomplete and is in no way a reflection on those places whose names do not appear below.

Walnut Acres
Penns Creek, PA 17862
(717) 837-0601

Good Food Store
920 Kensington
Missoula, MT 59801
(406) 728-5823

Ohsawa-America
PO Box 3608
Chico, CA 95927
(916) 342-6050

Jaffe Brothers
Valley Center, CA 92082

Westbrae Natural Foods
PO Box 8711
Emeryville, CA 94662
(415) 658-7521

Arrowhead Mills, Inc.
PO Box 2059
Hereford, TX 79045
(806) 364-0730

Mendocino Sea Vegetable Co.
PO Box 372
255 Wendling St.
Navarro, CA 95463

Ozark Cooperative Warehouse, Inc.
401 Watson St.
PO Box 30
Fayetteville, AR 72701
(501) 521-COOP

RESEARCH & THE GROWTH OF VEGETARIANISM 3

There is a long history of vegetarian cultures, including the Hunza, the Seventh Day Adventists, and various Indian sects. Among these communities, vegetarianism is firmly grounded in a cultural setting; sufficient nutritional knowledge is embedded within daily and yearly rituals, assuring continued health.

In the United States, the Seventh Day Adventists were the first large subculture to develop and maintain a healthy vegetarian life style. Foods were selected and eaten in accordance with religious principles backed by sound research at the Loma Linda University, renowned for its scientific studies of the vegetarian diet. Well-trained doctors provide the proper medical supervision for this vegetarian lifestyle; children's health has always been a priority.

The Seventh Day Adventists are lacto-ova-vegetarians; they consume milk and eggs as a common part of their diet. Studies of teens raised as Seventh Day Adventists show normal growth rate and no cause for concern about their health and diet.

In the late 1960's, another group of vegetarians, which researchers often called the "new" vegetarians emerged in the United States. Initially these vegetarians formed a homogeneous group, close in age, with relatively similar, non-vegetarian backgrounds. The first moves toward vegetarianism often came as part of a rebellion against the status quo; most of the new vegetarians were unable to turn to their parents for information that would support the new life style. Many rejected traditional medical and scientific systems in their search for a more holistic way of life.

Practically no research was done on children of these vegetarians until the early 1970's, because not until then did the new vegetarians begin having children. Early research in the 1970's often showed the biased attitude of the medical "establishment." Studies of single children admitted to hospitals for malnutrition "proved" that vegetarianism was not a healthy food choice. Titles of studies from this period reflect the bias: "A Starved Child of the New Vegetarians," "A Syndrome of Methylmalonic Aciduria Homo Cystinura, Megaloblastic Anemia and Neurological Abnormalities in a Vitamin B-12 Deficient Breast-fed Infant of a Strict Vegetarian" (whew!), or my favorite, "Nutrition in Infants Receiving Cult Diets: A Form of Child Abuse."

Members of the health profession held out this research almost as a threat to parents who might choose to raise their children as vegetarians, and it served little purpose except perhaps to arouse the curiosity of other researchers. But slowly the attitudes of researchers began to change, even if the results themselves were not too promising. The remaining research on vegetarian children in the 1970's consistently showed that children on strict vegan and macrobiotic diets exhibited signs of mild to severe malnutrition, and children on vegetarian diets of all kinds were apt to be lighter in weight and shorter in length.

Fortunately, in the 1970s, vegetarians began to educate themselves. A wide range of nutrition books, including the invaluable *Laurel's Kitchen* and *The Farm Vegetarian Cookbook*, appeared for the public. Magazines such as *Vegetarian Times* began publishing in the late 1970's, responding to the new vegetarians who were hungry for good information. A large Tennessee commune, "The Farm," began to produce cookbooks from their own experience with vegetarian families.

As vegetarians grew older and began to have children, they began to create a supportive culture for themselves. Cooking and gathering information about nutrition became respected occupations within the new vegetarian subculture.

Research began to reflect this new availability of nutrition information. In 1981, a study concluded that a vegan diet can indeed be a healthy diet for children if properly planned. Even before 1981, studies which still questioned the macrobiotic diet were endorsing a vegetarian diet for children which included some products such as milk, cheese, yoghurt, and eggs.

Even conservative institutions have come out with positive approaches to vegetarianism, as in the 1974 and 1980 position papers on vegetarian diets published by the National Academy of Sciences and the American Dietetic Association respectively. In 1986 the ADA also published a recommendation statement on the "Proposed Rule for Meat-Alternates Used in Child Nutrition Programs."

As a cultural group gains and retains nutritional knowledge, it begins to ensure its own survival. Severe malnutrition is now seen to be linked to a lack of nutritional knowledge by a particular set of parents, and not considered typical of vegetarian children. When groups of vegetarian children are studied, the differences from the norm get smaller through the years as nutrition information becomes increasingly available.

Perhaps, also, the fight against the "establishment" grows less meaningful as many new vegetarians of the 1960's become establishment age themselves in the 1980's. In fact, research suggests that this recent willingness to work with the medical scientific world has made vegetarianism less separate from the primary culture. Now that the National Academy of Sciences has published a list of Dietary Goals for the United States which reiterates many vegetarian principles, healthy vegetarian diets will surely be made available to more children. A little bit of cultural acceptance can go a long way.

The macrobiotic community, however, continues to maintain its separation from the mainstream medical and social cultures in the United States. Practitioners of macrobiotics often reject traditional medical information and supervision. Instead, the Eastern yin-yang philosophy on which it is based offers comprehensive principles for every area of daily life providing a cultural integrity of its own.

Macrobiotic and other strict vegetarian diets can be healthy for children, but to raise a child on such a diet without the aid of an educated community demands considerable effort. Research continues to show that macrobiotic children are more likely to have nutritional deficiencies than children on other diets, as well as significantly slowed growth rates.

Don't give up, though! If a parent is educated and stays in touch with someone well versed in macrobiotic nutrition and normal child development, normal growth and health can be achieved. Here are some good references on macrobiotic nutrition:

1. Macrobiotics International and the East West Foundation, 17 Station St., Brookline, MA 02147. (617) 738-0045

2. Kushi Institute, Box 568, 17 Station St., Brookline, MA 02147 1 (800) MACRO-17 (toll-free hotline for macrobiotic programs and services)

3. Kushi, Michio and Aveline. *Macrobiotic Pregnancy and Care of the Newborn*. USA: Japan Publications, 1983.

4. _____ . *Macrobiotic Childcare and Family Health*. USA: Japan Publications, 1985.

5. Weber, Gayle. *Macrobiotic Cooking for Children*. 2424 Aldrich Ave. S., Minneapolis, MN 55405.

Remember that books should be supplemental to continued contact with a person knowledgeable in nutrition fundamentals.

In the 1980's, pure foods and natural foods are the rage. "Yuppies" exemplify the new, economically secure food faddist who helped to create the enormous natural foods industry that exists today. In 1983, the *New York Times* used the header, "Pure Food: The Status Symbol of the Decade," to describe the atmosphere of this time.

Profiteers already exploit the market, repackaging foods to justify higher prices. In one of our local food cooperatives, concern over the exploitation of the health-food market causes active debate about stocking pre-packaged, small-portioned foods. A macrobiotic chef with a family of her own says she sometimes wishes there could be macrobiotic fast food. Time constraints of parenting and working make many parents reach for the higher-priced convenience "natural" foods. Unfortunately, foods may be pure without being nutritious, and every move away from preparing one's own meals removes direct control over one's diet. One store, described in the *New York Times* article mentioned above, aims to present itself as healthy, pure, and natural on the premise that people are tired of having to learn abut nutrition themselves and are more than anxious to have a store that promises to take care of all those nutritional details for them.

If you listen to a group of children talking, you won't hear much mention of nutrition. But as parents, we must not give up our responsibility for passing along sound nutritional information to our children. We are a vital part of a growing culture, learning to educate ourselves, with the power to share this knowledge with others. By communicating this information to our children, we perform one of the most powerful acts of all, because it is through this process that vegetarianism becomes embedded in our culture, to be "naturally" passed along through generations to come.

When Looking at Research

While investigating information for vegetarian parents, I ran into what I fondly think of as "the studies:" the research reports from the scientific community about a few vegetarian children over the last twenty years. Sometimes research findings can be a little scary, until you think twice and realize that they can be presented to prove just about any point of view.

In the beginning, "the studies" were confined to cases of children who were already sick. If someone ever tries to use one of these cases to suggest you should feed your child meat, after reading this chapter you will be able to calmly explain the difference between a study done twenty years ago and one done last year.

However, research does have its place. In the case of vegetarian children, it helps parents by pointing out the areas of nutrition which are most important to keep in mind for the growing child. Helpful, for example, is the knowledge that macrobiotic children must have good exposure to the sun as a source of Vitamin D if supplements are not used, or that the weaning period is a time when many vegetarian children get significantly fewer calories than they need for normal growth. A promising development in recent studies is that vegetarian children now rarely exhibit Vitamin B-12 and protein deficiencies. These deficiencies were the major scare factors I ran into as a vegetarian parent eight or ten years ago, but it seems that adequate nutritional information has been disseminated throughout the vegetarian community so that parents take care that the especially important needs for these nutrients are being met.

Since results often reflect the researcher's bias, they should be taken only as tendencies rather than law. Here are some guidelines that might help put a research study into better perspective:

1. When was the study published?
A study is published at least a year after the research is completed, and completion itself may come long after data is gathered. Think about the world when the study was actually done: how did most people feel about this subject at the time?

2. Where did the research take place?

It makes quite a difference if a study was done in a poor section of India where malnutrition is the rule or in a rich white suburb of Boston. A study which focuses on a child first encountered in the hospital is different from one which surveys normally healthy children in, for example, a preschool situation. Also, a study done in a community with strict religious guidelines which affect diet may be quite different than one done of vegetarians grouped more randomly by location.

3. How many children were included in the study?

The results of a study of one hospitalized child have very different implications than a study of seventy-five children leading normal lives. As a rule, the more children in a study, the more useful it is for the general public. A study of one child may provide clues as to the ways nutritional deficiencies manifest themselves, but will relate less directly to basically healthy children. Also interesting to note is the ratio of girls to boys studied. Although the Recommended Dietary Allowances for healthy growth are not separated by sex until age ten, some studies will include only boys. While we cannot know what information is falling through this gender gap, it is an additional variable that can tilt a study one direction or another.

4. Why was the research done?

In the beginning of a study, the author(s) usually give a background for the study and some basic premises—what they expected to find. In general, you can count on more objectivity from researchers who identify their premises. You may find a subtle anti- or pro-vegetarian stance by "reading between the lines."

5. What does the research suggest?

At the end of a research article, there is usually a "discussion" or summary of the research and its implications. This is where the feelings of the researchers appear. Research may be interpreted in many ways, as shown by a study of preschoolers in Boston that was reported by two different groups of researchers, each evaluating a different variable, but using the same data. One group looked at a narrow age range for growth rate patterns; the other looked at the wider range for vitamin D intake. The results do not contradict each other, but are a good example of how research can be used for different purposes.

The following pages contain information from eighteen studies of vegetarian children. The studies are listed by publication date, which may be up to several years after the research took place. I have included both the major findings as well as implications of the research. (In the next chapter I examine more fully the major concerns raised by this information.) This is virtually a comprehensive listing of research to date, except that I did not include studies of children in tropical climates living under very poor conditions.

1. Publication Date: 1973
Title of Study: "A Starved Child of the New Vegetarians"
# of Vegetarian Children: 1
Age Range: Not Available
Findings: The child showed severe malnutrition.
Implications: Maintain regular contact with a doctor or someone with medical knowledge to make sure your child is in good health.

2. Publication Date: 1974
Title of Study: "Zen Macrobiotic Dietary Problems in Infancy"
# of Vegetarian Children: 2
Age Range: 7-13 months
Findings: Both energy and protein intake were low enough to cause deficiency to the point of retarded growth.
Implications: Make sure the core foods the child eats are sufficiently high in protein and calories and that his diet is varied but well-balanced.

3. *Publication Date:* 1975
Title of Study: "Dietary Status of 'New Vegetarians' "
# of Vegetarian Children: 10
Age Range: 1-6 years
Findings: The weight and height of children on a macrobiotic diet fall enough below the acceptable standards to cause concern. The calcium and riboflavin levels are also too low.
Implications: Make sure a diet contains the recommended amounts of energy, protein, calcium, and riboflavin.

4. *Publication Date:* 1975
Title of Study: "Kwashiorkor in Chicago"
# of Vegetarian Children: 1
Age Range: 9 months
Findings: Kwashiorkor (severe malnutrition) was found in a child eating a pure vegan diet.
Implications: If your child is less than healthy, check with a doctor. Some children may not be getting adequate nourishment from the particular selection of foods provided and may need greater variety and quantity. (See the section in Chapter four on checking your child's health.)

5. *Publication Date:* 1977
Title of Study: "Velocities of Growth in Vegetarian Preschool Children"
# of Vegetarian Children: 72
Age Range: 6 months-5 years
Findings: Vegetarians up to 6 months showed normal growth; from 6-18 months growth was slower than average; from 18 months to 5 years, some children showed growth spurts and regained their normal growth expectancies. Macrobiotic children were more likely to show growth spurts during the 18 month-5 year age range.
Implications: Since some children did not have the 'catch-up' growth spurts that normally occur during the 2-5 year range, it is important that the protein/calorie intake during the 6-18 month period be great enough to avoid an early slowdown in growth rate.

6. *Publication Date:* 1978
Title of Study: "Preschoolers on Alternate Lifestyle Diets"
# of Vegetarian Children: 119

Age Range: birth-5 years
Findings: Children between the ages 6-17 months showed signs of slowed growth in all areas except head circumference. The older the child, the more serious the problem.
Implications: Keep an eye on growth rates; check with a doctor on a regular basis and modify the diet if needed.

7. *Publication Date:* 1978
Title of Study: "Seasonal Variations in Preschool Vegetarian Children's Growth Velocity"
# of Vegetarian Children: 51
Age Range: 15-18 months
Findings: Vegetarian children grew most slowly during the spring and summer months, which is the opposite of the norm, where the greatest growth spurts occur in the spring.
Implications: Make sure children get enough protein and carbohydrates during the spring and summer months as well as enough vitamin D (sunlight/supplement) during the winter to build reserves for growth.

8. *Publication Date:* 1978
Title of Study: "A Syndrome of Methylmalonic Aciduria Homo Cystinura, Megaloblastic Anemia and Neurological Abnormalities in a Vitamin B-12 Deficient Breast-fed Infant of a Strict Vegetarian"
# of Vegetarian Children: 1
Age Range: under a year
Findings: The child showed severe malnutrition and growth abnormalities.
Implications: The breast-feeding mother should make certain that her vitamin B-12 intake is adequate. Check regularly with a doctor to be sure that the child's growth is normal and that he is not severely ill. (I suspect that such a severe illness would be apparent to most parents, especially those who are part of a vegetarian community.)

9. *Publication Date:* 1979
Title of Study: "Risk of Nutritional Rickets among Vegetarian Children"
# of Vegetarian Children: 52
Age Range: birth-6 years
Findings: Macrobiotic children were found to show an increased

risk of rickets due to an inadequate vitamin D intake combined with low calcium and phosphorus intake.

Implications: Make sure children on a macrobiotic diet receive sufficient sun exposure or vitamin D supplement (100 IU daily). Also watch calcium and phosphorus intake.

10. *Publication Date:* 1979
Title of Study: "Multiple Nutritional Deficiencies in Infants from a Strict Vegetarian Community." (The group involved in this study was a religious vegan community.)
Number of Vegetarian Children: 4
Age Range: 5-13 months
Findings: The children showed severe protein/calorie and vitamin B-12 deficiencies.

Implications: If your community is limited, make sure well-balanced meals are provided and that the child's growth and health are monitored regularly by a qualified medical person able to work within your dietary guidelines.

11. *Publication Date:* 1980
Title of Study: "Mental Age and I.Q. of Predominantly Vegetarian Children"
of Vegetarian Children: 28
Age Range: 1-7 years
Findings: Children on a vegetarian diet (including 17 macrobiotic children) had "superior performance" on the Stanford-Binet Intelligence Test; physical development was within the normal range.
Implications: A relatively high level of education of the parents may have been crucial to the positive results in this study. Parents should be encouraged to keep learning about nutrition—it's paying off in smart, healthy children!

12. *Publication Date:* 1980
Title of Study: "Size, Obesity, and Leanness in Vegetarian Preschool Children"
of Vegetarian Children: 142
Age Range: birth-3 years
Findings: The length of all the children was less than the norm for the age with macrobiotic children showing mild malnutrition.
Implications: Make sure a weaning diet (6-35 months) is adequate, especially in carbohydrate intake.

13. *Publication Date:* 1980
Title of Study: "Preschool Vegetarian Children"
# of Vegetarian Children: 48
Age Range: 2-5 years (at "The Farm")
Findings: The average nutrient intake, except for calcium, was adequate even though the children were a little slimmer than the norm.
Implications: A vegan/vegetarian diet can meet the RDA's for children when meals are properly planned.

14. *Publication Date:* 1981
Title of Study: "An Anthropometric and Dietary Assessment of the Nutritional Status of Vegan Preschool Children"
# of Vegetarian Children: 23
Age Range: 1-5 years
Findings: The vitamin B-12 and iron intake was adequate. The children tended to be smaller and lighter than the norm. Energy, calcium, and vitamin D intake were below the RDA. "Vegan diet can meet nutritional needs if sufficient care is taken."
Implications: Educated meal planning is important to the success of a vegan diet. Watch energy, calcium, and vitamin D intake.

15. *Publication Date:* 1982
Title of Study: "Nutritional Status of Vegetarian Children"
# of Vegetarian Children: 39
Age Range: preschool
Findings: Vitamin D intake was 1/8 of the RDA in macrobiotic children.
Implications: Make sure vitamin D intake is adequate, either through exposure to the sun or with a vitamin D supplement.

16. *Publication Date:* 1983
Title of Study: "Growth in 'New Vegetarian' Preschool Children Using the Jenss-Bayley Curve-Fitting Technique"
# of Vegetarian Children: 142
Age Range: 6 weeks-6 years
Findings: Vegetarian children were found to be 0.5-1 kg lighter and 1-2 cm shorter as a group when compared to the norms. Females and those children on a macrobiotic diet had the lowest weight and height in the group. Energy intake was low, but protein intake was adequate.

Implications: Monitor growth rates (use charts in chapter four) especially during the 1-3 year range. Make sure your children get adequate vitamin D. (For the most part, the children tested fell within the accepted range for growth rate, but careful meal planning is needed to insure continued growth.)

17. *Publication Date:* 1985
Title of Study: "Relationship of Vegetarianism to Child Growth in South India"
# of Vegetarian Children: 627
Age Range: 0-6 years
Findings: Vegetarianism was positively associated with growth in economically poor communities for children over three years. (Perhaps high-income families who could afford to buy meat relied less on nutrients from non-meat sources.)
Implications: Vegetarianism is a healthy and economically viable diet.

18. *Publication Date:* 1985
Title of Study: "Food Consumption and Height/Weight Status of Dutch Preschool Children on Alternative Diets"
# of Vegetarian Children: 92
Age Range: preschool
Findings: Vegetarian children ate diets closer to the RDA's than meat-eating children. Macrobiotic diets were low in calcium, vitamin D, and riboflavin. Cereals were the most important source of energy and nutrients.
Implications: Watch the calcium, vitamin D, and riboflavin intake in macrobiotic diets.

This summary of scientific studies of vegetarian children can point out to us some of the key concerns we must have in providing our children with a nutritionally complete, healthful diet. At the same time, the studies alone could be overly alarming unless they are taken in context. Please re-read the commentary, "When Looking at Research" on pp. 72-75, earlier in this chapter.

Bookstores and libraries have shelves overflowing with books on nutrition, with endless charts on what vitamins and minerals one needs to be healthy, what foods contain these nutrients, and how to prepare foods so that scientific information becomes tasty. With this overload of nutrition information, it is easy for parents to feel doubts at times as to whether their children are eating properly. The idealism of the parent-to-be may be abruptly grounded by the eccentric eating habits of a real child, who does not care for gourmet casseroles in which taste and nutrition are perfectly combined, doesn't like new foods, or is allergic to certain foods.

A basic knowledge of nutrition *is* essential for every parent. In this chapter we'll look at the health issues raised by nutrition research, along with some common concerns of parents, and I'll give methods of checking your child's health yourself.

RDA's—
Recommended Dietary Allowances

There are actually two meanings to the term RDA. One is the *Recommended Dietary Allowance*, established by the Food and Nutrition Board of the National Research Council. This body meets once every few years (the last two reports were in 1974 and 1980) to establish "recommendations for the average daily amounts of nutrients that (healthy) population groups should consume over a period of time." Established primarily for those living in the United States, these recommendations have two main limitations:

Major Nutrient
Recommended Daily Dietary Allowances*

Nutrient	Ages 1-3	Ages 4-6	Ages 7-10
Weight (lbs)	29	44	62
Height (in)	35	44	52
Energy Needs (kcal)	900-1800	1300-2300	1650-3300
Protein (g)	23	30	34
Vitamin A (μg RE)	400	500	700
Vitamin D (μg)	10	10	10
Vitamin E (μg α-TE)	5	6	7
Vitamin C (mg α-TE)	45	45	45
Thiamin (mg)	0.7	0.9	1.2
Riboflavin (mg)	0.8	1.0	1.2
Niacin (mg NE)	9	11	16
Vitamin B-6 (mg)	0.9	1.3	1.6
Folacin (μg)	100	200	300
Vit B-12 (μg)	2.0	2.5	3.0
Calcium (mg)	800	800	800
Phosphorus (mg)	800	800	800
Magnesium (mg)	150	200	250
Iron (mg)	15	10	10
Zinc (mg)	10	10	10
Iodine (mg)	70	90	120

* From: *Recommended Dietary Allowances*. 9th ed. National Academy of Sciences. Washington, DC. 1980.

1. RDA's have not been established for all the essential nutrients.
2. Interactions among nutrients are not always known and cannot be accounted for when defining the recommended amount for a single nutrient.

The book, *Recommended Daily Allowances*, published by the National Research Council on RDA's, is fascinating reading. It explains how and why the committee reached decisions

Additional Nutrient
Recommended Daily Dietary Allowances*

Nutrient	Ages 1-3	Ages 4-6	Ages 7-10
Vitamin K (μg)	15-30	20-40	30-60
Biotin (μg)	65	85	120
Pantothenic Acid (mg)	3	3-4	4-5
Copper (mg)	1.0-1.5	1.5-2.0	2.0-2.5
Manganese (mg)	1.0-1.5	1.5-2.0	2.0-3.0
Fluoride (mg)	0.5-1.5	1.0-2.5	1.5-2.5
Chromium (mg)	0.02-0.06	0.02-0.08	0.03-0.12
Selenium (mg)	0.02-0.08	0.03-0.12	0.10-0.3
Molybdenum (mg)	0.05-0.1	0.06-0.15	0.10-0.3
Sodium (mg)	325-975	450-975	600-1800
Potassium (mg)	550-1650	775-2325	1000-3000
Chloride (mg)	500-1500	700-2100	925-2775

* From: *Recommended Dietary Allowances*. 9th ed. National Academy of Sciences. Washington, DC. 1980.

concerning the Allowances. It does not hesitate to point out how little is really known about nutrition, and it acknowledges that their recommendations are usually slightly higher than necessary for many nutrients so that a wider variety of people can be included in the recommendations. Recommended Dietary Allowances are not designed for individual diagnosis by any means, since everyone varies tremendously in terms of body weight, energy output, and general health on any one day. RDA's are primarily guidelines for evaluating diets and preparing nutritional counseling guides for groups of people.

The second meaning of RDA is indicated by the prefix "US." In 1972 the Food and Drug Administration developed the United States Recommended Daily Allowances for use in nutritional labeling to help consumers in their food purchases. USRDA's replaced the Minimum Daily Requirements (MDR's) which had been used for many years previously on the labels of vitamins, some breakfast cereals, and other special foods. When the Food and Nutrition Board of the National Research Council developed the Recommended Dietary Allowances (RDA's), it defined the nutritional needs for fifteen different age categories including both sexes. However, in order to maintain simplicity in packaging, only a single set of USRDA's is used for labeling most foods. To assure a USRDA high enough for everyone, then, the levels were set using the highest allowances found in the RDA's.

Remember that neither the RDA's nor the USRDA's are a precise measurement of the nutritional needs for a particular individual on a particular day. Both are only *recommended* allowances.

To find out more about either of these, write:

1. *Recommended Dietary Allowances.* 9th ed. 1980. Food and Nutrition Board, National Academy of Sciences. Office of Publications, 2101 Constitution Ave. NW, Washington, DC 20418.

2. *US Recommended Daily Allowances: Nutrition Labels and US RDA's.* DHEW Publication No. FDA 76-2042. Office of Publications, 2101 Constitution Ave. NW, Washington, DC 20418.

Energy and Carbohydrates

During the weaning period (12-35 months), energy or caloric intake is often too low, which means that although a child may be eating a balanced diet she may not be eating enough food.

Carbohydrates are a good source of increasing energy. When I was researching *Vegetarian Baby*, one of my biggest surprises was the emphasis by a nutritionist who advised me that "carbohydrates are good for you." I had firmly linked carbohydrates with obesity—cut down on carbohydrates, I

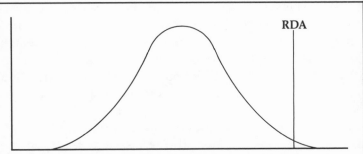

The Recommended Dietary Allowance is set high enough to account for the needs of 98% of healthy people.

From: National Center for Health Statistics

Mean Heights and Weights and Recommended Energy Intake

Category	Age (years)	Weight (kg)	(lb)	Height (cm)	(in.)	Energy Needs (with range) (kcal)	
Infants	0.0-0.5	6	13	60	24	kg x 115	(95-145)
	0.5-1.0	9	20	71	28	kg x 105	(80-135)
Children	1-3	13	29	90	35	1300	(900-1800)
	4-6	20	44	112	44	1700	(1300-2300)
	7-10	28	62	132	52	2400	(1650-3300)
Males	11-14	45	99	157	62	2700	(2000-3700)
	15-18	66	145	176	69	2800	(2100-3900)
	19-22	70	154	177	70	2900	(2500-3300)
	23-50	70	154	178	70	2700	(2300-3100)
	51-75	70	154	178	70	2400	(2000-2800)
	76+	70	154	178	70	2050	(1650-2450)
Females	11-14	46	101	157	62	2200	(1500-3000)
	15-18	55	120	163	64	2100	(1200-3000)
	19-22	55	120	163	64	2100	(1700-2500)
	23-50	55	120	163	64	2000	(1600-2400)
	51-75	55	120	163	64	1800	(1400-2200)
	76+	55	120	163	64	1600	(1200-2000)
Pregnancy						+300	
Lactation						+500	

From: National Center for Health Statistics

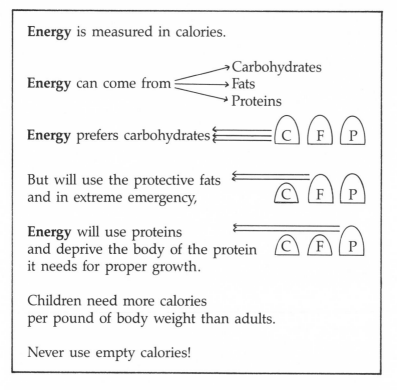

Energy is measured in calories.

Energy can come from → Carbohydrates
→ Fats
→ Proteins

Energy prefers carbohydrates C F P

But will use the protective fats C F P
and in extreme emergency,

Energy will use proteins C F P
and deprive the body of the protein
it needs for proper growth.

Children need more calories
per pound of body weight than adults.

Never use empty calories!

thought, and you'll be thinner and healthier. That was a misconception.

In general, eating unrefined (whole grain, unprocessed) carbohydrates and starches will produce a healthy energy intake.

Starches is the term used for complex carbohydrates, which break down into sugars during digestion. *Natural, unrefined* simple carbohydrates such as raw apple and banana provide fructose, a form of energy that does not alter the blood sugar level significantly. On the other hand, complex carbohydrates such as potatoes, parsnips, and even carrots release sugar into the blood stream almost immediately. Fruit sugars, beans, and peanuts are examples of foods that do not affect blood sugar as rapidly, but provide a "time-released" effect.

(A good source of further information about foods and blood sugar levels, which may be of particular importance to those with hypoglycemia or diabetes, can be found in: David Jenkins, Thomas Woelver, et al. "Glycemic Index of Foods: A Physiological Basis for Carbohydrate Exchange." *Amer. J. of Clinical Nutrition*, 34:362-366, 1981.)

Children who grow more slowly than normal during the weaning period do seem to grow more quickly during the preschool years (ages three to five), often re-establishing normal weight and growth patterns. This growth may be due to the wider variety of foods a child eats when in day care. Children at this age also begin to favor sweet foods, which may provide a beneficial increase in their carbohydrate intake, as long as the foods are nutritious. But bear in mind that extremely slow growth during the one to three-year-old period may be irreparable. In any case, it is wise to check your child's growth rate at regular intervals, even if she is in good health.

Know what the RDA's for energy are for your child's age (see table on page 86).

Estimate your child's caloric intake. This estimation should be relatively easy since at this age the child's diet is usually still under the parent's eye, or at least known.

Use the health parameters described in this chapter (pages 106–114) to see if your child falls within the normal ranges.

Have a medically knowledgeable person (e.g. a doctor) check your child's growth at regular intervals, especially if you have any particular concerns.

Calcium

Vegetarian diets for children, especially macrobiotic, tend to be low in calcium and sometimes low in zinc. Zinc can be found in sunflower seeds, mushrooms, nutritional yeast, and soybeans. Calcium is not as available in plant foods as

Patties

Whether you call them patties, croquettes, or burgers, this food form is loved by most children, especially when served with catsup. Serve patties with a whole grain muffin or bread and a salad or vegetable for a complete meal that your child will be sure to eat.

Patties can be made in bulk and saved for quick baking or frying. The main difference between patty mixture for baking and patty mixture for frying is that baked patties should have precooked ingredients. Grains and legumes used for fried patties can be uncooked but should be finely ground so they will cook properly in oil.

The basic patty mixture uses the following ingredients:

1/3 cup legumes   1 cup grain   1 1/3 cups grain
1/2 cup seeds   or 1/3 cup seeds or 1/2 cup legumes

Add nut butters, an egg, a little oil, or tahini to make a patty texture.
Add spices (oregano, garlic, soy sauce, onion powder) for taste.
Add bread crumbs for a lighter texture.

Store ground grains, legumes, and spice mixtures in tight fitting containers. Add nut butters or other cohesive elements only when you are ready to fry the patties. For a nutritional crunch, bread the patties with vitamin B-12 enriched yeast flakes before frying.

Store patties for baking (which should be made from cooked grains, beans, and legumes) in final patty form in zip lock freezer bags in the freezer for a prepared meal any time. Cover patties with cheese when baking, or bake in aluminum foil to preserve texture.

Ideas for Patty Mixtures

Lentils, sunflower seeds, almonds
Carrots, brown rice, peanut butter
Millet, brown rice, pumpkin seeds
Lentils, walnuts, oatmeal
Barley, millet, cashews
Soybeans, tahini, bread crumbs
Garbanzo beans, celery, sesame seeds

Homemade Catsup

Mix: 1 cup tomato puree (6-8 tomatoes cooked and
      pureed)
    1/2 cup olive, soy, or safflower oil
    1 tablespoon vinegar (or more, to taste)
    1 tablespoon honey
    1/2 tablespoon lemon juice
    1/4 teaspoon onion powder
    1 dash soy sauce (to taste)

Blend well, varying ingredient amounts to reach desired
consistency.

It's amazing how many things children will eat with catsup!

in animal foods. To get the same calcium found in one cup
of milk, you would need to eat one of the following:

1 cup broccoli, collards	1 cup almonds
1 1/4 cup turnip greens	1 1/2 cups kale
1 2/3 cup sunflower seeds	2 cups beet greens

3 cups cooked dried beans

Calcium is essential to health, especially for bone growth
and for teeth. Canada and the World Health Organization
recommend lower calcium RDA's than the United States, as
shown below:

Calcium Needs

	US RDA	Canada RDA	W.H.O. RDA
Ages 1-6	800 mg	500 mg	400-500 mg
Ages 7-10	800 mg	700-800 mg	400-600 mg

Calcium works interdependently with phosphorus. If phosphorus intake is too low, the body will not be able to absorb calcium properly. The RDA for phosphorus for the United States is 800 mg/day, while the Canadian RDA is 500 mg for ages 1-6 and 700 mg for ages 7-9. The calcium/phosphorus combination is important, rather than the total amount of each consumed separately.

Some good sources of phosphorus include whole grain breads and cereals, nuts, beans, and legumes. Notice that nature has planned well: calcium and phosphorus are plentiful in the same kinds of foods, guaranteeing that they will be eaten in the proper quantities at the same time.

Remember that too much of anything isn't good for you or your child!

Vitamin B-12

Vitamin B-12 is essential to proper development and the health of the central nervous system. One of the biggest concerns of vegetarian parents has been providing their children with adequate levels of B-12, which is almost entirely unavailable in vegetables. Over the years, however, several new sources of vitamin B-12 have been introduced to the vegetarian community and B-12 deficiency is no longer a serious threat to vegetarian health in this culture. This change does not mean, of course, that we can ignore the body's need for vitamin B-12. As in *Vegetarian Baby*, I recommend that vegan parents give their child nutritional yeast with B-12 or a supplemental B-12 vitamin. On a regular basis check with your

Salads

Salads are not usually the food of choice for children, but if they accompany meals on a regular basis, a healthy habit may begin at any age. Children often prefer fresh raw vegetables to cooked ones, which tend to lose much of their nutrient values in the cooking process.

For younger children, especially, the texture of a salad is very important. A salad that takes a long time to chew may not be chewed well. Large leafy vegetables can take up much unwelcome psychological space on a child's plate. Use a grater or shredder, or finely chop vegetables to make a more compact and edible salad for children.

Some leafy vegetables are high in oxalic acid. Oxalic acid binds calcium and iron, which makes it harder for the body to absorb them. Since calcium is so important to proper bone growth and formation in children, avoid spinach, chard, parsley, and beet greens except as an occasional dish.

Another way to reduce the binding effect of oxalic acid is to provide an acidic environment; add a little fresh lemon or orange juice to a salad dressing or directly to the top of the salad itself. Tomatoes also add acidity to a salad.

The following vegetables are high in calcium and low in oxalic acid. They can be finely grated or chopped into salads, which should be served often.

| mustard greens | turnip greens | dandelion greens |
| collards | kale | green lettuce |

Other healthy salads for children include the following, all finely grated:

    Carrot and cabbage salad with apple or pear
    Cucumber, carrot, and celery salad
    Kale and carrots and a few raisins

Broccoli stems with carrot and celery
Crisp diced dandelion greens and chopped tomatoes
Cottage cheese with any chopped vegetables or fruits
Sprinkle a few sunflower or sesame seeds on top for older children.

doctor for the proper amount for your child's age, weight and dietary needs.

Vitamin B-12 is found in tempeh, dulse and kombu (two varieties of seaweed), in many fortified soy products, and in dairy products. The recommended daily dietary allowances for B-12 are as follows:

Children 1-3 years	2.0 micrograms/day
4-6 years	2.5 micrograms/day
7 and up	3.0 micrograms/day

The macrobiotic philosophy as presented by Michio Kushi (the leading teacher of macrobiotics in the United States) suggests 5.0 micrograms per day of vitamin B-12 for adults and uses seafoods, tempeh, and miso as sources of this essential nutrient. In addition, Kushi states in his book, *The Macrobiotic Way*, that B-12 is often found in harmless bacteria or molds on the skins of organic fruits and vegetables. If food is grown in healthy soil and processed minimally before eating, it will retain small but significant amounts of B-12.

Non-macrobiotic vegans and vegetarians would be wise to follow Kushi's suggestion and include sea vegetables in their diets. Sea vegetables are extremely high in B-12. Asakusa Nori, for example, has approximately 13 micrograms of B-12 in each 100 grams of its dried form. Since the RDA for B-12 never exceeds 3 micrograms per day, this vegetable is obviously a good source. The B-12 content of other kinds of seaweeds is around 6.3 micrograms per 100 grams of their dried form.

Sea vegetables are also high in iodine, iron, vitamins A, B-1, C and E, protein, and calcium. The following are some sea vegetables available in many health food stores:

Agar-agar	Kelp
Arame	Kombu
Dulse	Nori
Hijiki	Wakame

Sea vegetables can be shredded over a grain dish, cooked with other vegetables, used to make a soup stock, or simply added to soups. Some seaweed, such as nori, comes in thin, dried sheets and can be used to wrap rice balls or make noodle rolls. Other seaweed—kombu for example—is also dried but retain its frond-like leaf shape.

Vitamin D

Vegetarian children of all kinds grow most slowly during the spring, with macrobiotic children showing the slowest growth rates. This pattern is opposite to that of children on a meat diet, and out of line with nature's pattern; living things usually grow more, and more quickly, in the spring than in any other season.

One reason for the slowed growth rates may be a lack of vitamin D in the diet, since vitamin D is essential to proper use of calcium, as in bone development, for example. Possibly during the colder months, when children are less likely to be exposed to the sun, vitamin D reserves are depleted, so that growth in the spring months cannot depend upon stores built up during the winter. When days begin to shorten, regularly use vitamin D supplements, fish oils, or soy milk fortified with vitamin D, if your child has less exposure to the sun. Do let your child play outside as much as possible, for sunlight on the skin enables the body to make its own vitamin D.

Juices

Drinking vegetable juices can be an easy way for children to get calcium, B vitamins, and minerals. A powerful blender that changes vegetables into juices is an expense that will pay for itself nutritionally very quickly. Ask for one as a gift if you can't afford one, or be on the lookout for sales in the newspapers. Less efficient machines create pulpy liquids which children may be more likely to reject, and straining out that pulp is wasteful.

The nutrients mentioned in the juices below are not necessarily found in store-bought prepackaged juices. Even homemade juices lose nutrients if they sit around, so a freshly made juice is the best!

Beet Juice contains a generous amount of sodium, and also iron, calcium, potassium, and vitamins A, B, and C.

Cucumber Juice is a rich source of vitamin C, potassium, iron, and magnesium, with some vitamins A and B.

Cabbage Juice contains vitamins A, B, and C, calcium, and iron.

Carrot Juice contains vitamin A, potassium, magnesium, iodine, and phosphorus and is a very good source of easily absorbed iron and calcium.

Celery Juice is high in magnesium and iron, with some potassium, calcium, and vitamins A, B, C, and E.

Dandelion Juice is an excellent source of magnesium, with many other minerals such as calcium, chlorine, phosphorus, and iron.

Kale Juice is a very good source of vitamin A, calcium, riboflavin, iron, and potassium.

Lettuce Juice, made from the darker green lettuce varieties offers a good supply of potassium, calcium, chlorine, phosphorus, iron, magnesium, and vitamins A, B, C, and E. The darker green lettuce, often bitter to the young palate, is more acceptable when mixed with carrot and celery juices.

Sprout Juices, whether you use bean, alfalfa, or legume sprouts as a base, are rich in protein, usable calcium, B vitamins, and iron—often with a delectable sweetness!

Tomato Juice is rich in magnesium, iron, potassium, phosphorus, calcium, iodine, vegetable amino acids, and vitamin C.

Vitamin Supplements

This letter describes a fairly common situation:

"My daughter, Shannon, is six months old. She is breast-fed and eating bananas, pears, yogurt, and rice cereal plus wheat germ and some juice. She was put on Tri-Vi-Sol vitamins, an A, D, and C supplement, which was fine. But last month, when our doctor found out we were vegetarians, he gave me another type. You need a prescription for it! It is Tri-Vi-Flor, a vitamin and fluoride combination. The fact that I need a prescription scares me, and I don't feel this fluoride is necessary. But no one seems to have an answer. A dentist friend of ours feels it's not. Meanwhile, I'm not giving them to her at all."

Doctors may tend to prescribe vitamin supplements if they aren't familiar with vegetarian diets. In general, healthy children do not need vitamin supplements. Vegans, however, should be especially careful about getting enough vitamin B-12 and may need to use supplements. More helpful to this mother would have been for the doctor to have sought information about what makes up a healthy vegetarian diet and then gone over the girl's actual diet before making any recommendations for supplementation. If the child were not healthy, the doctor could have helped the mother to determine what nutrients might have been missing and supplied them with vegetarian foods. It *is* possible!

But there are times when vitamin supplements may be necessary. Every child is different, and some may not be getting enough of a particular nutrient from their diet. These children may become ill unless their diet is supplemented in some way. Some children can be allowed to miss meals or to ignore certain foods because they are getting sufficient nutrition from the rest of their meals. Note, however, that because a particular vitamin or mineral is necessary for say, healthy nervous system development, more is not necessarily better. Vitamin supplementation should *only* take place after a diet has been thoroughly examined by a nutritionist or a doctor and found wanting.

Recently, an article in *American Health* magazine demonstrated the kind of complications that can occur with nutritional supplements. Apparently, infants and children who can't tolerate milk are sometimes prescribed bone meal or dolomite supplements to assure adequate calcium intake. However, lead and other minerals are concentrated in these supplements and can produce numerous side effects, all bad, which will affect the health of the child. The FDA recommends that such supplements be kept low if needed at all. Alternate sources of calcium, such as blackstrap molasses, carob, green vegetables, and tofu, are a much healthier approach.

A study reported in the April 1983 issue of the American Dietetic Association's magazine examined the nutrient and food supplement practices of lacto-ova vegetarians. 85% of the sampled population used food supplements ranging from 100% to 15000% of the RDA in additional nutrients to the diets. An analysis of the diets of this group, excluding supplements, indicated *no need for vitamin supplementation*; the diets were all well-balanced and healthy without it. The supplements were taken, according to the report, without clear and specific rationales by the users. The most frequently cit-

11 Meals Children Will Eat

1. Ramen noodles with tofu chunks and peas (as soup or casserole)
2. Macaroni and cheese and peas (any noodles with cheese sauce)
3. Oatmeal with wheat germ, raisins, and cinnamon
4. Pasta (spaghetti or any whole grain pasta) and tomato sauce (Add well cooked soy grits for extra flavor and nutrition.)
5. Cottage cheese with peas and a whole-grain bread with a nut spread
6. Burger/patties with whole-grain roll, catsup, and salad
7. Rice and nuts/seeds with vegetable side dishes
8. Pizza (whole grain crust spread with tomato puree, oregano, and cheese)
9. Tofu scrambled eggs (Mash tofu to scrambled egg-like consistency. Mix with egg or a little tahini, a dash of soy sauce or cheese. Cook like scrambled eggs.)
10. Whole grain pancakes with grated vegetables in the batter, served with applesauce or sour cream
11. Potato pancakes with wheat germ (Grate potatoes and an onion. Mix in an egg, a little pepper, and 1/3 proportion of wheat germ. Fry like a patty. Serve with catsup or sour cream on top, with a salad on the side.)

ed reason for use of supplements was to make up for what's not in food," and yet the dietary analysis indicated no such deficiencies.

Vitamins and other nutrients work together in a balance not completely understood by researchers. More is *not* better, and can even be dangerous if toxic levels are taken or if a higher dosage of one nutrient throws off the balance and proper use by the body of other elements.

A Support System That Works

A child can be deficient in an important nutrient without the parents immediately recognizing it; a basically healthy child must use up stored nutrients before malnutrition or retarded growth appear. While these reservoirs are available in emergencies, they should not be regularly depleted; it is like running low on gas without a gas gauge. It is important not only to educate oneself as a vegetarian parent, but to have the trained medical assistance and supervision all parents need.

Parents need cultural support. All vegetarian parents should have the right to nutritional advice from a doctor who is knowledgeable enough to respect vegetarianism. As this diet becomes a more common choice, I hope that more doctors will educate themselves on the subject so that no longer will there be medical problems among vegetarian children due to ignorance and lack of community acceptance. Until that time, however, it may be necessary to educate your doctor yourself. This offer won't always be well-received, but you must have a doctor who either accepts vegetarian diets or is willing to learn about them, even if it means finding a new doctor. We all need doctors who respect our life choices, particularly when those choices, like vegetarianism, are based on solid research and nutritionally sound principles.

Find people in your community who have either nutritional or medical knowledge or both. Naturally, doctors who are themselves vegetarians are ideal, but if such a doctor is not available, find at least one person whose knowledge and training you respect.

Maintain contact with this person or people. The best book cannot give as specific a response to your child's needs as can someone who examines her in person.

Try to be part of a vegetarian community, and help build it by adding both information and questions. If we work together, knowledge will travel faster and assure health for more vegetarians.

Dental Health

Normal Development

Tooth development follows a predictable pattern, but because heredity is an important factor as well, the *rate* of development will vary from child to child. The following information is based on averages. If your child's teeth develop more slowly or more quickly than other children the same age, find out your own tooth development pattern before becoming concerned about the variation.

Baby teeth begin to develop about 7 1/2 months before birth. Adequate calcium intake and a good diet are therefore essential for the mother during pregnancy. The front incisors, the first baby teeth, begin to appear when the child is between three and nine months old. Usually the lower teeth start to come in before the upper teeth.

Twenty baby teeth are in place by the time the process is completed at around age two. There are three kinds of baby teeth:

1. Incisors (8)—cutting
2. Canines (4)—tearing (also called cuspids)
3. Molars (8)—grinding

When a child is around three years old, the roots of these baby teeth begin to dissolve gradually. By the time the permanent teeth are ready to surface, the roots of the baby teeth have completed their job of preparing the way for the larger teeth. This process is less painful for the child than the eruption of the baby teeth which had to tear the skin.

Permanent teeth also begin to develop prenatally, although most of the growth takes place after birth. The first permanent teeth to emerge are the first molars, right behind the baby teeth. Since these also break the skin and usually erupt between the ages of five and seven, they are often called the "six-year-molars." Until the age of twelve or thirteen, a child will have a combination of baby and permanent teeth. It is fitting, somehow, that a child's baby teeth are not all gone until the time adolescence starts.

By age seventeen, twenty-eight of the thirty-two permanent teeth will have appeared. The final four, often called "wisdom teeth" (to tease people who are older when they get them, and compliment those who are younger), often arrive by the mid-twenties. These back four teeth have really become vestigial; humans have not lived on hunks of raw meat for a long time now, and so we are slowly developing a twenty-eight-toothed skull.

Cavities

A tooth has three main parts:

1. Pulp—the center of the tooth which is soft and made up of nerves, blood vessels, and connective tissue.
2. Dentin—a hard yellow substance (harder than bone) that covers the pulp. This is what we usually think of as tooth.
3. Enamel—a thin, white, but transparent covering over the dentin. Enamel is the hardest tissue in the body and the final shield for the pulp.

How a cavity forms
Saliva makes a thin invisible film on the tooth.
Food bits and natural mouth bacteria stick to the film (plaque).
Acid is formed when the bacteria digests the food particles (especially the carbohydrates!). Then the acid begins to dissolve the enamel if it is not removed by flossing or brushing. After that, it eats through the dentin and into the pulp

if it is not treated. Once it hits the pulp, nerves are affected and a toothache occurs.

Caring for Teeth

- Encourage your children to rinse out their mouths after eating any snacks. This simple habit can make a great deal of difference in keeping the mouth clean. If your child is shy about this procedure in a public place, or if it would indeed be inappropriate for the occasion, suggest just drinking some water and swishing it around gently in the mouth before swallowing. Remember, even juices and sodas are snacks!

- Buy a soft, child-sized toothbrush when your child is around the age of 2 1/2-3. Show your child the three sides to the teeth that heed to be brushed—the front, back and top. Establish a habit in a comfortable manner, since you are practicing on the baby teeth, which will fall out.

- Take your child for a dental visit around the age of three. Find a dentist recommended by other parents, or whom you know and like. This should just be an initial check up for the dentist to determine that jaw formation is proceeding normally. It is also a chance for the child to be with a dentist in a relatively relaxed atmosphere.

- When your child is around the age of five (earlier if the child has the agility and you have the patience), introduce her to flossing. It may already have been a topic of conversation as she observed you flossing your own teeth regularly!

  Flossing cleans in between the teeth where one tooth touches the next—the areas which aren't reached by brushing. If teeth are irregular, there may be particular places where food is likely to collect. The dentist should be able to point out these places.

- After flossing and brushing, children should rinse out their mouths with water. This process removes the dislodged food, bacteria and plaque.

- Go to the dentist for regular checkups, usually once every six to nine months.

Making Your Own Toothpaste

Modern toothpastes often contain sweeteners, colorings and chemicals that you may not want to use. These extra ingredients which give a brand its particular color, texture and taste, are rarely listed on the package. The law requires that only the active ingredients appear on the label.

While there are natural alternatives on the market, such as Tom's brand and Dr. Bronner's liquid cleansers, you might enjoy making your own toothpaste with your child. It is a little bit like making a "potion"—something that children love—and the process can give you an opportunity to explain about proper tooth care without lecturing abstractly.

Toothpaste or tooth powder keeps teeth and gums healthy in several ways. For example, although most modern toothpastes have a creamy texture, the traditional tooth powder is slightly abrasive. The base of most tooth powders is *precipitated chalk* or *calcium carbonate*, which will clean the enamel without scratching it.

Because chalk or ground calcium carbonate are not terribly tasty, *essential oils*, such as peppermint, spearmint, or wintergreen, can be added to make the flavor more acceptable to children. (Television commercials often use this fact, truthfully saying that if children like the taste of the toothpaste they will brush more often.) Essential oils combine well with the chalky texture of the base materials to provide a smoother taste without reducing the necessary roughness of the chalk. The oils also have antiseptic qualities.

Because essential oils are concentrated, you will need only a drop or two for every four to six tablespoons of chalk. If you prefer the mixture to be more like toothpaste than powder, add a little water. Essential oils evaporate, so be sure to keep the mixture in a sealed container.

You can also add *soap powder* or *cream of tartar* to provide foam or fizz that not only improves the texture, but reaches into and helps clean, the crevices between the teeth.

Experiment with these ingredients, using the amounts suggested above as a starting place. Don't make too much of any mixture until you find something that is right for you.

Teeth and Nutrition

Good nutrition goes hand in hand with brushing, flossing, and regular visits to the dentist. The most important nutrients for proper tooth formation are calcium, phosphorus, and vitamins A, D, and C.

- Raisins are as bad for your teeth as candy. Whether a sugar is natural or refined makes no difference in the process of cavity formation. Dried fruits are extremely sticky, cover a large are area of the teeth, and create a perfect environment for tooth decay.

- Chocolate is one of the least harmful sweets for your teeth. It contains oils which prevent bacteria from sticking to the enamel. The sugar in chocolate may not be good for your body, but it isn't very harmful to your teeth.

- Refined carbohydrates are worse for your teeth than whole grains. Refined carbohydrates are easier for bacteria to eat, causing plaque to build up faster.

- Repeated exposure to sugars increase the chance of developing cavities. Keep snacking to a minimum, supervised amount. Random, all-day access to snack foods, no matter how good they are for a child nutritionally, can be terrible for teeth. A mid-morning and mid-afternoon snack, followed by brushing or rinsing the mouth, is probably the best plan for children who can't last until the next meal (in other words, *most* healthy children!). Remember to have your child brush after a bedtime snack.

• Sucrose (what we commonly mean by sugar) is more harmful to teeth only because of the relatively high consumption compared to other sugars. In fact, fructose (fruit sugar) has been found to be as harmful and perhaps even more so because of the acidic properties of fruits which can destroy the tooth's protective enamel.

Fluoride

I became aware of the controversy of fluoridation by reading a little book called *How Dangerous is Fluoridation*, published by Free Men Speak, Inc. Today it is a prevalent concern: fluoridation does not enter a community's water source without public debate. While the fluorides that occur naturally in water significantly decrease the incidence of cavities in people drinking that water, not everyone approves of fluorides being added as chemicals to water supplies.

In 1945, a community in New York and another in Michigan began to fluoridate their water supplies in response to research that supported the use of fluoridated water in producing healthier, longer-lasting teeth. By 1950, results showed that the incidence of cavities had decreased in those communities and United States public officials issued a national recommendation for public fluoridation of water. Today, the public water supplies of about half the people in the United States are fluoridated.

People become concerned about the practice of fluoridation when it was discovered that large doses of fluoride could cause tooth and bone damage. Many believed that there was too much fluoride in their water supplies. Several communities have actively campaigned against fluoridation.

A good alternative to fluoridating a community's entire water supply is to have a doctor prescribe a small dosage of fluoride for your child. That way, your child's teeth can have the protection fluoride does give, without the risk of an overdose.

Check with your local public health offices to find out if your water is fluoridated, and to what extent. If there is no fluoridation, consult with your dentist. If your water is fluoridated naturally, don't worry. Since many public health officials and dentists consider fluoridation to be beneficial, involving little or no risk, I recommend keeping yourself informed and following the topic in the news.

Checking Your Child's Health

After reading about nutritional deficiencies in children who appear to be healthy, you may wonder how you can be sure that your own child is getting what she needs. How can you be sure that a child is not dangerously depleting stored nutrient reserves, when you can't tell just by looking?

Most parents recognize when a child has the flu or some other ordinary childhood sickness. The child will be full of energy one day and listless the next, often with a very hot head and maybe no appetite at all. Any sign of fever indicates that the child's body is fighting infection, and parents can be alerted by these relatively straightforward signals of illness.

Severe malnourishment will also be obvious with so many pictures of starving children filling the media to remind us. However, mild or chronic malnutrition which is not a result of extreme poverty may not have obvious symptoms. It may, in fact, take several months and sometimes even years for a specific deficiency to become severe enough to be noticeable. If a deficiency shows up gradually in a child, it may not easily be noticed by the parents and other close relatives and friends. A gradual lessening of energy, for example, might look like a slight mood or personality change.

Given the results of research on vegetarianism, it makes sense for vegetarians to check their own children's health. Although the methods described in the next few pages cannot take the place of medical checkups by experienced practitioners, they can provide early warning signals to parents. Any information that parents can give a doctor will help with more accurate diagnosis if a concern arises.

When you take your child to the doctor for a "well child" visit (nothing is wrong; you are just making an annual check-in), the doctor will probably measure the following:

Height	Weight
Head circumference	Arm circumference
Triceps skinfold thickness	Subscapular skinfold thickness

Because growth is very sensitive to inadequate nutrition, these measuring tools are crucial. Triceps and subscapular skinfold thickness tests are not always done during a check-up, but are useful for determining the amount, type and tone of fat tissue on the body. Precise measurement of head circumference is difficult since the variation from normal to abnormal is quite small. The major indicators of normal growth, however, are height and weight—measurements that are easily accessible to parents. Arm circumference is useful for parents as an indicator of moderately severe malnutrition.

Measuring Height and Weight

The National Center for Health Statistics has developed charts to show the ranges of height and weight for children in the United States. Studies of different ethnic groups suggest that these standards are valid for cultures throughout the world.

Remember, when comparing your childs growth to the average, that vegetarian children tend to be shorter and lighter than the norm as a group. If your child is slightly under average, there may be no need for concern. Also, if you (the biological parents) are a little shorter or lighter, you can expect the same to be true of your child.

Vegetarian children rarely have to worry about being over-weight, but parents do need to be alerted if a child is markedly underweight and does not gain the normal amount each year. A reduction in the rate of weight gain (fewer than 3-4 lbs/year) is a cause for concern, as is continued low weight. A *severely* underweight child is malnourished and likely to suffer some brain damage.

Height and weight are dependent on three main factors:
—Genetic make-up (the height/weight of the parents)
—Nutritional adequacy during the growing years
—Exposure to diseases during the growing years

Most childhood illnesses that affect height can be prevented by proper immunizations.

To measure your child's height, take all measurements without shoes or thick socks. For children under the age of two, height measurements are usually taken with the child lying down. To measure your child's weight, use a reliable scale and take all readings with the child wearing minimal clothing.

Step 1: Record your child's measurements every birthday.

	height	weight			height	weight
1 year:				6 years:		
2 years:				7 years:		
3 years:				8 years:		
4 years:				9 years:		
5 years:				10 years:		

Step 2: Enter the information on the height and weight charts in this chapter. You can practice on the chart below.

Example: A five-year-old is 39″ tall. You would enter the in-formation as shown on the chart below. The dotted lines are only to show you how to place the dot. The same child has

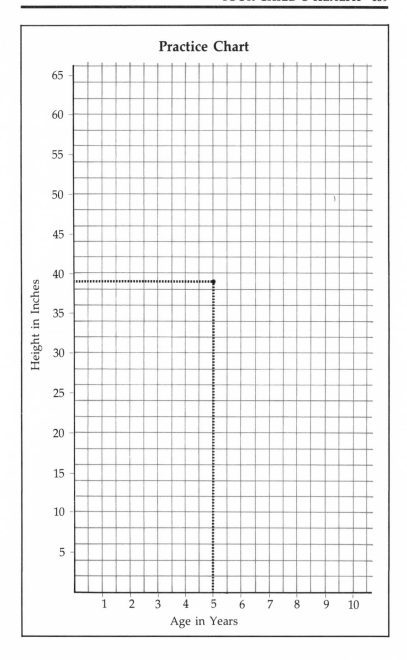

Practice Chart

Height in Inches

Age in Years

Rules of Thumb

A child's birth length usually doubles by age four.
A child's birth length usually triples by age thirteen.
You can expect a child to be twice as tall as an adult as
she is at age two.

---

the following readings up to the time she is six years old.
Enter them on the chart and connect the dots to show the
child's growth pattern for height.

2 years—34"	4 years—37 1/2"
3 years—36"	6 years—42"

If you had entered this information on the height chart in
this chapter, you would then be able to compare it to the
growth patterns of other children. The lowest line (5%) indicates that fewer than 5% of all children are shorter than
heights indicated by a dot on this line. The highest line (95%)
indicates that only 5% of all children are taller than heights
indicated by a dot on this line.

The 50% line is considered average. Thus, if a child has
a height line lower than this, she is considered slightly at risk
for malnutrition and her diet should be checked.

The *rate* of growth is also important. If your child gets taller
by 2-3"per year, and heavier by 4-6 lbs per year, the growth
rate is considered normal.

Arm Circumference

Arm circumference is the measurement around the upper
part of the arm. Measuring the mid-upper arm can be a quick
way to assess moderately severe malnutrition, since undernourishment will cause body fat to disappear and muscles
to lose tone. This area grows fastest during the first year of
life as muscles and body tone develop. From 1-5 years, meas-

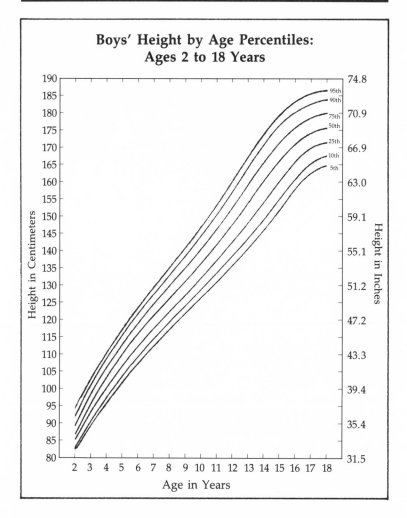

Boys' Height by Age Percentiles:
Ages 2 to 18 Years

urement of arm circumference is usually stationary at approximately 6 1/2″ (16 cm).

A reading of 5-5 1/3″ (12.5-13.5 cm) is considered a sign
of moderate malnutrition. A reading below 5″ (12.5 cm) is
considered a sign of severe malnutrition.

If concern arises, check arm circumference measurements
with someone knowledgeable about the procedure.

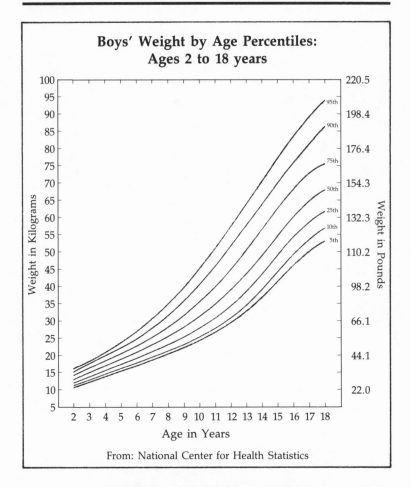

**Boys' Weight by Age Percentiles:
Ages 2 to 18 years**

From: National Center for Health Statistics

Should I Worry?

If you take a child for an annual checkup, the measurements described in this chapter will be part of the regular procedure and will go into a medical history record. The doctor will mention variations from normal growth, and you can make adjustments to diet as needed.

If you do not take your child for an annual checkup, be sure to keep records as suggested in this chapter. In addi-

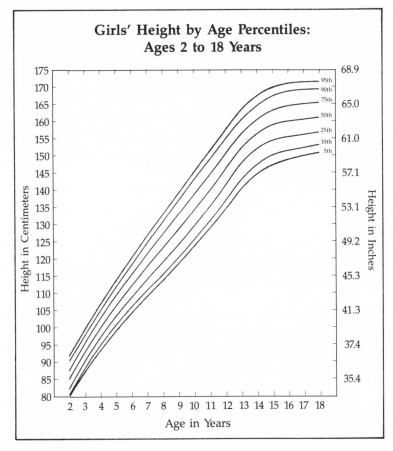

Girls' Height by Age Percentiles:
Ages 2 to 18 Years

tion, the following questions may help you notice possible problems:

1. *Is your child regularly underweight or small for her age?*

2. *Has your child's weight or height rate of growth changed over the years? (If your child grew normally or even fast and then slowed down, keep a record of the changes.)*

3. *Is your child regularly tired or listless? Does she lack energy?*

4. *Does your child often seem unhappy (e.g., cries easily for no reason, seems depressed, becomes difficult to get along with)?*

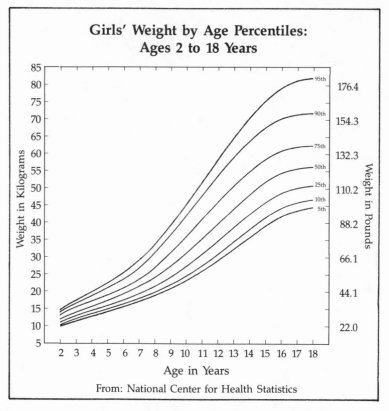

**Girls' Weight by Age Percentiles:
Ages 2 to 18 Years**

From: National Center for Health Statistics

5. *Does your child have frequent infections or other complaints about health (stomachaches, headaches, constipation, diarrhea)?*

When in doubt, it's "better to be safe than sorry." Find medical help if you are worried.

Sometimes knowing too much can make a parent feel that there are too many things to worry about. Relax! If you are familiar with a child's nutritional needs and give the child meals that meet these needs, she should not only be healthy in the present, but building a strong and resilient body for the future.

MORAL DEVELOPMENT 5

F or many of us, vegetarianism is rooted in respect for animal life. Others may adopt the vegetarian diet out of respect for their own bodies' health. Both reasons may be present; often what begins as an experiment or a stand taken on a single issue grows into a broad-based philosophy of life. Personal values may come from, or lead to, a larger commitment to health and life on the planet.

Parents naturally want to pass on a certain moral perspective to their children. Moral values are the principles by which we decide what is right and wrong. Moral maturity is the ability to see and weigh ambiguous factors when such a decision must be made. Vegetarian parents hope to see their children grow to become vegetarians by their own choosing, rather than because Mom and/or Dad says so. This desire leads to two important questions:

Do children have the same reasons adults do for being vegetarian? Can the ethical nature of vegetarianism be taught?

Research in how moral reasoning develops can lead parents to a better understanding of their children. We can better communicate with our children if we compare their behavior to some general behavior patterns. Evidence shows that moral judgement and behavior do mature over time. This finding does not mean that a child begins as an immoral being and becomes in time a moral adult, but rather that the reasons a child does something seem to be different than the reasons an adult does the same thing. The child's reasoning is not wrong, but does not exhibit the broader base of knowledge and experience that come into play in an adult decision.

This is not to say that there is a single moral perspective that is the hallmark of maturity. Even as adults we find ourselves in some situations where "right" and "wrong" may not be clearly distinguishable. For example, it is difficult for some vegetarian parents when a grandparent offers the child meat; the desire to assert one's right to raise a vegetarian child may clash with the desire to let the child (especially an older one) make his own decisions. Some parents give priority to a smooth relationship among all three generations and others value vegetarianism and its implications more highly. What is clearly right to one parent may not be clearly right for another parent. This ambiguity is difficult to face and difficult to tolerate.

Perspectives of Major Researchers

In the 1930's, Swiss psychologist Jean Piaget observed children as they played games, noting how children at different ages respond to rules. For some children the rules were Law; for others, rules were constantly changed and argued so that at times it seemed that the children were playing the game primarily for the purpose of figuring out the rules. He also studied children's criteria for right and wrong, and their notions of fairness.

Up to age two, according to Piaget, children might play a game, but rules are almost useless; only the simplest rules can be understood, and the children are content to go where their curiosity takes them. Between the ages of two and six, children begin not only to understand rules exist, but to consider them untouchable: even when disobeying, a child will not question them. Rules come from outside—parents, older siblings, etc.—and are obeyed by imitation, from a desire to please, or from prodding. Changing the rules will disturb a child in this age group. Fairness seems to be determined by the judgement of parents and other adults.

Between the ages of seven and ten, children better understand that rules are essential to the proper playing of a game, and they manifest a strong internal drive to obey them. When questioned about the rules, children in the study showed gaps in understanding details, but this lack of complete comprehension did not shake their belief in the importance of the rules.

At the end of this period and on into preadolescence children are more concerned with having a clear understanding of rules. A child at this age may question the rules and even try to change them. Some he will have assimilated and will not question. Fairness, for children in the eight to twelve range, is bound up in equality, which is strictly defined; extenuating circumstances are unimportant by comparison.

The work of Lawrence Kohlberg, begun in the 1960's, defines moral development further and somewhat differently than Piaget's. Using a series of moral dilemmas in which there are no clear answers, Kohlberg talked with children at different ages and in a wide variety of cultures. He suggests six stages through which people may advance. He also distinguishes between moral behavior and moral judgement; the moral standards by which we claim to live are often belied by our actions.

Kohlberg admits that not all people go through all the stages, and certainly not at the same rate. It is not possible to say, for instance, that a four-year-old will be at stage one and should progress to the third stage by the time he's ten.

We can move through a stage and then return to it, or even operate in more than one at once.

Kohlberg's system shouldn't be used alone to measure a child's moral maturity. Until recently his theory was taught as if it applied to all of us, when in fact it is based on a study of eighty-four boys. Carol Gilligan's study of the moral development of girls and women, begun in the 1970's, shows that women think differently about moral questions than do men. Where men tend to see moral questions in terms of individual rights that can be objectively established and agreed upon, women generally think in terms of relationship, care, and responsibility. Girls tend to choose cooperative games such as jump rope, while boys are interested in more competitive games. Because they frame the whole notion of morality differently, the moral development of women is not the same as that of men, and moral maturity must be measured differently.

Gilligan's theory has found possible confirmation in a study of vegetarian children done in 1983 by Johanna Dwyer. This study, primarily to assess the health of vegetarian children with varying diets, found that vegetarian girls tended to adhere to much stricter diets than boys, eating fewer animal foods. While boys were more likely to drink milk and eat other animal products (cheese, eggs) when away from home, girls were more disciplined on their own, suggesting that a commitment to a vegetarian diet was an easier and more binding value for the girls.

This research does point out that this strictness can be detrimental to the girls' health, as the girls in question were lighter and thinner than other girls of the same age. Perhaps parents of vegetarian girls should be especially aware of respecting the girls' choices while at the same time assuring that they receive adequate carbohydrates and proteins from acceptable sources.

No doubt other critiques of Kohlberg will be forthcoming, giving us a wider picture of human values. Nevertheless,

Kohlberg's stages provide a useful structure through which we may look at moral questions.

Kohlberg defines three different levels of moral development, each of which contains two of the six stages referred to above. In the following pages, I have combined interviews with vegetarian children with a description of each of Kohlberg's stages to answer the question, "Why are children vegetarians?"

Kohlberg's Stages of Moral Development

1. The Pre-Conventional Level

A. The External-Control Stage. A child does something because his parents say so. There is no questioning and, in the child's mind, no difference between what the parents say is right and what he believes to be right. The following conversation is typical of a child at this stage:

Q — Do you eat meat?
A — No.
Q — Why don't you eat meat?
A — Because my mommy doesn't eat meat either.
Q — Do you know why she doesn't eat meat?
A — Because it's bad.
Q — Why is it bad?
A — My mommy says it's bad.
Q — Do you know why she says it's bad?
A — No.

B. The Instrumental-Relativist Stage. The child does something to satisfy personal desires, without thinking about the effects of his actions. He is beginning to recognize his own interests, a first step in autonomy.

Q — Do you eat meat?
A — Sometimes.

Q—What makes you eat meat sometimes and not other times?
A—Sometimes I like it and sometimes I don't.
(If a conversation at this stage is pursued, the child will often return to the earlier stage under pressure.)

2. The Conventional Level

A. *The Interpersonal-Relationship Stage.* "Right" is pleasing others and doing what they approve. Stereotyped behavior and a desire to conform are strong during this stage. If family values conflict with those of the world outside the home, the child may resolve it by acting one way with parents and another way outside the home to try to be "good" on all bases.

Q—Do you eat meat?
A— Well, when I'm home I don't because my parents are vegetarians, but if I'm at Ron's house, then I do because they have hamburgers there.
Q—Do you think it's okay to eat meat sometimes?
A— Well, it's not okay at home. But when I'm at Ron's house and his parents say it's okay, then it seems like it's okay to me, too.

Other children may resolve the split by relying on their families; the need to please their parents may be stronger than peer pressure.

Q—Do kids ever tease you about being a vegetarian?
A— Well, they ask me why I don't eat meat and I say because I'm a vegetarian.
Q—Then what do they say?
A— They say, "Oh!" Half of them don't even know what a vegetarian is! My mom says I should ignore them.
Q—Do the kids think vegetarians are strange?
A— Yes, but I don't mind, because my dad said everyone thought the Wright Brothers were strange, but look where it got them!

B. *The Social-Maintenance Stage.* The child is increasingly oriented towards becoming a part of society. He shows a strong sense of loyalty and commitment towards a larger group. At this stage, a vegetarian community of friends helps to offer a child an alternative society with which to identify. If a family is too isolated, the child may ignore family values in search of a larger society.

Q — Do you eat meat?

A — No, and neither does Sue or Melody.

Q — Why not?

A — Well, we don't think you should kill animals to get food.

Q — What happens if you go out for dinner and there isn't much to eat except meat?

A — Oh, that's no problem. At Sue's house, her Mom cooks meat, but she'll let us make our own dinner if we want to and sometimes she even makes us vegetarian food! My family always has Thanksgiving dinner with other vegetarians anyway, and so we don't care if other people eat meat.

Q — You don't care if other people eat meat?

A — No, but sometimes we invite some friends over who aren't vegetarians to show them what we eat, and they like it, well, most of the time.

3. The Post-Conventional Level

A. The Social-Contract Stage. The person becomes involved in creating a life style developed from moral principles that have been agreed upon by a group. Kohlberg feels that few people ever progress to this stage; most are content to have their society's predetermined laws function as ultimate guiding principles and do not seek to go beyond them. This group could easily include those vegetarians who have worked over the years to make vegetarian nutritional principles useful to a wide variety of people, making the vegetarian world more accessible to all.

B. The Universal-Principle Stage. Here "right" is not limited by society, but still takes into account the health and welfare of all. Kohlberg reserves this category for only a few: Jesus Christ, Buddha, Martin Luther King, and Gandhi. Understanding this level is difficult, admits Kohlberg, since it is so rare and cannot be observed and documented easily.

The work of both Piaget and Kohlberg suggests that young children will be vegetarians not because they share their parents' reasoning, but because they have not yet seriously begun to question or try to adjust rules. If vegetarianism is a way of life for a family, chances are it will be taken for granted by a young child. While the child may be curious about other foods, vegetarianism itself will not likely be questioned.

Naturally parents will be pleased if their children accept vegetarianism with little resistance, and rightly so—it's wonderful to see your child eating well, especially while he is still growing. From the standpoint of moral development, however, it's important even at an early age to begin to talk about the life choices that vegetarianism implies. Habit is a strong foundation until it becomes something to rebel against; if your child becomes grounded over the years in the many areas of life that vegetarianism touches, he may rebound more quickly from youthful rebellion to a healthy life style.

Dialogue appears to be much more effective than insistence. Older children, exposed to other life styles, will begin to question with increasing detail. They may be looking for answers from their parents to help escape peer pressure, they may be filling in gaps in their own knowledge, or they may be purely curious. Piaget's research suggests that a period of questioning precedes the ability to make a mature moral decision. Questions are a healthy sign, allowing the child a chance to test doubts and values. For us as parents, giving our children both objective and subjective information as part of a dialogue (rather than a harangue) may be the best thing we can do to help our children in their development.

Here are some questions that can begin to open up the philosophy behind vegetarianism for your child. Choose those that are appropriate for you and easily understood by your child. This is not a catechism; if you introduce the subjects one or two at a time in appropriate circumstances (while cooking, shopping, gardening, etc.) you may find that you awaken interest and deepen your child's understanding of this aspect of your lives.

Do you know why we are vegetarians?
Where do vegetables come from?

What is the difference between chain grocery stores and smaller natural foods stores?

Why are packaged foods more expensive? What is packaging?

Why do people eat meat?

What foods do we buy that are grown locally?

What foods do we buy from out of the state/country?

When are foods in season? Why might it be preferable to eat foods in season? What are special foods for the fall, winter, spring and summer?

What kinds of foods do our grandparents and other relatives eat?

How can we introduce vegetarian foods to our meat-eating friends?

What do you do when someone thinks the food you are eating is strange?

What makes a vegetarian diet healthier than a meat-centered one?

How can a vegetarian diet save you money?

Who are some famous vegetarians? Do you think people make fun of what they eat?

Prohibition

Parents often wonder about the effect of prohibiting their children from eating meat and junk foods. Does prohibition make something *more* or *less* desirable? If young children don't have an adult moral perception and are not ready for abstract concepts, doesn't simple prohibition make sense? If a child grows up in a house where meat and sweets are restricted, what happens when the child grows old enough to make dietary choices without parental permission or knowledge?

One parent talks about his son:

"I guess there was something close to prohibition when my son was under six. Although there was nothing that we completely banned, we discouraged certain things very strongly. At that point, he was very receptive and sensitive to our desires. But I didn't believe that the way to develop his own self-discipline was simply to impose rules on him. I observed several other families where there was outright prohibition, and in many of these situations I saw active resistance from the children; the food became a forbidden fruit that they would seek out or fantasize about, make jokes about behind their parents' backs.

"At this point, my son is thirteen and I feel that he has to take some responsibility for making his own decisions. When he was younger, I would be fairly quick to offer my opinion when other people offered him foods I didn't like him to have. Now, I can feel disappointed if he chooses to accept foods that are obviously not nutritionally good for him, and sometimes I'll make a comment, but I don't put a lot of emphasis on it. I'll talk to him about why I eat the way I do, and I try to set an example whenever I can, but at this point his diet is his own choice."

Dan Hoffman, Ithaca, NY

A fascinating study of toy preference and prohibition was done by Aronson and Carlsmith in 1965. A toy that was somewhat desirable to the children was forbidden during free play time, with a strong threat attached: if the child touched the toy during that time, some severe form of punishment would occur. When the children were later allowed to play with a variety of toys, including the forbidden one, it became the preferred toy and the interest level was still very high. However, when the toy was forbidden during free play with only a mild threat, the toy became less important when the children were later allowed to play with it. This lowered level of interest lasted over time.

Although this is an experiment with toys rather than food, the implications are important: if meat or junk food is forbidden with a severe threat attached, children are more likely to continue to have a high level of interest in it. However, if adults issue only a mild reprimand, the food may become less important.

In the study, adults always voiced their feelings on the subject. Children need and will respond to guidance; the question is how heated the verbal guidance should be. If a threat is too mild, the child may doubt the parent's sincerity or concern with the prohibition. If the threat is too strong, the child will probably temporarily revert to accepting the parent's judgement as right and his own as wrong. This deterrence won't decrease the "wrong" behavior, except perhaps when the parent is watching. Remember that moral dilemmas do encourage moral development if the child is allowed the freedom to make a decision.

What a child wants will of course not always be what the parents want. Talking about it, giving him your opinion without enforcing it by brute authority, and encouraging him to give reasons for his actions will help your child develop a moral conscience. All parents must face the fact that their children will grow up with some different values than they had hoped to instill. Moving from parents' complete control over the diet of their young child to their lack of control over a teenager's diet is a big step.

"Our seven-year-old is developing a desire to try what all the other children eat. He often voices a yearning for fish— he wants to know what it tastes like. We have resolved the situation by saying we won't have fish at home, but that he can make his own decision when we go out for a meal where fish is available. So far, he has had several opportunities, but each time has chosen not to eat fish.

"At home we have only vegetarian, nutritious foods, and we hope that our influence stays with him. We have done our best to give him a strong healthy body in his early years. But somewhere out there when he's on his own for much of the time, he is going to start experimenting for himself.

"We have many values that differ with those of our parents, and our children will make their own decisions also. We feel that we can give our children guidance, a good start, and then let them go their own way, while asking that they respect our own strong convictions."

David and Ruth Gaillard, Hardwick, VT

Parents *do* have the responsibility for their children's diet, especially early in life. Providing a caring and proper home with a healthy vegetarian lifestyle is not essential to moral development. Such a home, however, will provide many powerful resources to our children as they grow older and make their own choices in the world.

For a school-aged child beginning to feel peer pressure, vegetarianism will probably not be the most important issue. If you can bring your child up in contact with a community of like-minded people, you'll be able to alleviate some of the pressure of feeling caught between two worlds. Children who are raised as vegetarians may share the same attitude as their parents about using animals for food, and may be above average in nutritional awareness and understanding, but they have not made for themselves the decision to be vegetarians. Just as any other moral stance develops, experience, education, and separation from one's parents play an important part in mature reasoning and moral behavior.

Children who are not raised from birth as vegetarians, but who become so as part of a change in family eating style, are likely to be more ambivalent about vegetarianism, since for them it is experienced as an often difficult move away from the norm. Parents need to include these children at each step along the way. Reasons for choosing vegetarianism can range from emotional to economic to environmental, and parents can be resources as well as moral guides.

This issue brings us back to the question of whether the ethical nature of vegetarianism can be taught. I think that most vegetarian parents agree that there is a natural appeal to the concept of not eating meat, which suggests that understanding of the ethical nature of vegetarianism could develop naturally in a supportive environment. The main thing to remember is that the supportive environment is important; children do not easily accept ideas that are forced on them, but their sympathy can be engaged if the process is gentle. By providing children with information, rather than dictums, and allowing them to make their own decisions as they grow older, you will encourage receptiveness to the ideas you wish to pass on.

SOCIAL RESPONSIBILITY 6

Social responsibility and moral development are closely linked. You can tie your understanding of vegetarianism into other ethical issues such as animal rights, world hunger, environmental safety, or local community action. Moral development is a maturing of values so that one's personal actions become meaningful within the context of the community and the "whole earth." Social responsibility is moral development in action.

In a child's earliest years, the parents' primary role is to provide a healthy environment for her. Most activities center around the basic physical care of the infant, and her exposure to new concepts and first time experiences. Parents may find themselves focused on the activities in the home during their children's first years. Most feel that they just haven't enough time for much besides parenting and work.

However, as the child grows older, able to walk around, less needy of the parents' constant attention, and able to play with other children and less adult supervision each year, little bits of free time and energy usually emerge. While parents will need to use much of this free time for their own relaxation and adult interests, it can also be the beginning of sharing a sense of social responsibility with the child.

Being a vegetarian brings one into contact with a variety of social issues, from animal liberation to ending the possibility of nuclear war, to combatting famine and hunger throughout the world. Many of these issues require people with tremendous time and energy to do the necessary work, and parents may shy away from involvements which would take too large a toll on family life.

But our children are our future, and by acquainting them with some of these issues in concrete ways, we can have an enormous effect from our own homes. As a mother employed full-time outside the home, I certainly understand limits on time and energy, but have found that some issues seem important because of my child, and so it is a little easier to find extra time.

In the following pages, I have listed a few areas that parents might want to explore with their children. Here are some useful questions for considering these issues:

1. *Why is this issue important to me as a parent?*
2. *In what ways does this affect my child?*
3. *What does my child know about this issue already?*
4. *What kinds of things would I enjoy doing with my child that relate to this issue?*
5. *How can we incorporate some aspect of this issue into our daily lives?* (This item is important in the light of the almost faddist approach to many social problems where the newest issue easily replaces an old one.)

Animal Rights

Young children don't really understand death, but they love animals and are often protective of them. They don't like the idea of killing animals, even though they may not have the slightest idea what that means. The natural empathy children and perhaps most people of all ages feel towards animals can be a starting point for talking about vegetarianism and animal rights.

Children seem to understand where meat comes from once someone explains. I do not think it is necessary to expose young children to the horrors of how some animals are readied for food, but the connection can be clearly stated. At age six, my son wanted to go through a supermarket and look at all the kinds of meat; while he thought it was "gross," he was still curious. I answered his questions with little added comment, because I felt that he was learning to make the connection between live animals and the packaged foods in front of him. It is too easy for most people to pick up the packaged food with little thought to the animal it came from.

An active animal liberation movement exists in the United States as well as throughout the world. Concerns of the groups range from protesting scientific experiments on animals, to identifying the use of animals and animal by-products in daily life. In the home, providing natural foods to your pets may be an easy first step. The following resources will help you get started:

1. Amberwood, Route 1, Box 206, Milner, GA 30257, (404) 358-2991.

Sells a wide variety of health and household items that are free of animal by-products.

2. *The Animals' Agenda*, published by The Animal Rights Magazine, PO Box 5234, Westport, CT 06881.

3. Curtis, Patricia. *Animal Rights*. Four Winds, 1980.

4. Magel, Charles. *A Bibliography on Animal Rights and Related Matters*. University Press of America, 1981.

5. O'Connor, Karen. *Sharing the Kingdom: Animals and Their Rights*. Dodd, Mead, & Co., 1984.

6. Singer, Peter. *Animal Liberation*. Avon Books, 1977.

7. _____ . *In Defense of Animals*. Basil Blackwell, 1985.

8. *PETA News*, published by People for Ethical Treatment of Animals, PO Box 42516, Washington, DC 20015. (Free newsletter—ask your local health food store to order it.)

World Hunger

With so many television extravaganzas and serious documentaries on the subject, it is impossible not to know that widespread hunger and famine exist throughout the world and within the United States. While many of us grew up being reminded of all the starving children in China, India, or Africa when we didn't want to finish our dinners, I'm not sure that these admonitions ever made any of us more socially responsible.

World hunger is such a vast concern that you may find it most practical to approach it in the home and your town first. Helping a child to understand where food comes from by planting a garden can be an important first step in her learning about the process of food distribution. Other ideas for teaching elementary school-aged children about this issue include "adopting" a hungry child, learning about hungry people in your own area, helping out at a soup kitchen (once, or even once a month), or simply beginning to learn about geography.

Again, it is not necessary to expose all the horrors of world hunger to a child; children possess a natural sensitivity. One of the most important messages to give them on this subject is that *something can be done*. Feeling hopeless or shocked from seeing hundreds of starving children on the evening news does not produce change. Taking small, active measures within our homes and communities, with our children, will make a difference.

Useful Resources

1. Austin, James. *Confronting Urban Malnutrition.* Johns Hopkins, 1980.

2. Beeghly, Leonard. *Living Poorly in America.* Praeger, 1983.

3. Leinwald, Gerald. *Hunger and Malnutrition in America.* Franklin Watts, 1985.

4. Oxfam America (resources for food and nutrition education), 302 Columbus Avenue, Boston, MA 02116

5. Schwartz-Nobel, Loretta. *Starving in the Shadows of Plenty.* Putnam, 1981.

Environmental Safety

Learning about environmental safety is a way of learning to separate health from hype. With children, it can be almost a game; you can check the ingredients on cereal packages, or try to figure out how big businesses, including the burgeoning health food industry, trick people into buying merchandise.

The major problem that parents may encounter when introducing their children to the distinction between health (safety) and hype (advertising, immorality in business) is the growth of cynicism. Studies show that children who watch television from the time they are very young quickly develop a high level of cynicism. This mindset occurs, perhaps, because advertisements never live up to what they promise. A similar attitude can arise in children who are taught about the "evils" of big business from an early age.

Indoctrination, even in the cause of good nutrition and vegetarianism, can backfire with young children who learn the rules and then apply them harshly to others. A vegetarian child, for instance, may publicly call attention to the poor nutritional habits of an elderly relative, or be derogatory to a person who is following different rules. As a parent, you should remember that when a young child is voicing opinions, a lack of respect for other people is as detrimental to a peaceful world as is eating meat or sugar.

There is an almost infinite number of environmental safety issues to consider with your children. The most effective place to start is in your own home, with things that your child encounters daily.

Some Project Ideas

1. Recycling

2. Conserving energy

3. Natural alternatives to poisons/chemicals

4. Growing your own organic food

5. Waste disposal, composting

6. Identifying animal products in household items

Helpful Books

1. Environmental Action to Coalition. *It's Your Environment: Things to Think About—Things to Do.* Charles Scribner's, 1976.

2. Lewin, Esther and Birdina. *Growing Food: Growing Up.* Ward Ritchie Press, 1973.

3. Paul, Aileen. *Kids Outdoor Gardening.* Doubleday, 1978.

4. Silverstein, Alvin and Virginia. *The Chemicals We Eat and Drink.* Follet, 1973.

5. Woods, Geraldine and Harold. *Pollution.* Franklin Watts, 1985.

Community Action

Making your own local community a healthier place is a more realistic starting point for a child than is concern with larger and more complex issues such as "the paradox of hunger in America" or "the social impact of malnutrition in the world today." Becoming involved in your community every week or two could be a special event for your family and an educational experience for your child. In my community, the options are unusually rich due to a large vegetarian "subculture." Families can work their own garden plots in a community garden site, be a member of a natural foods cooperative, go on an edible foods hike, or work with almost any day-care center to increase natural-foods awareness.

Other families may have to work a little harder to achieve community involvement. It may mean starting a natural-foods cooperative, having informal nutrition classes taught by the vegetarian cooks in your area, joining the Board of Directors of the nursery school your child attends, or having potluck dinners with other vegetarians to create your own supportive vegetarian community.

A lot depends on the family's free time, but if you can form even the smallest new connection between your family and the community in which you live, your values will have some influence. This process will not only give your children a sense of community and its inter-relatedness, but will also teach them that their involvement can make a difference.

Suggestions:

1. Help your children and other vegetarian children start a newsletter with their favorite vegetarian recipies and anecdotes.

2. Offer to bring natural-food snacks to your children's school or day care once a month (or more often, if you have time).

Organize other interested parents to help so that this sharing can happen once a week. (Thanks to my son's first teacher for this idea!)

3. If your help is requested for a school event, offer to set up a vegetarian booth which could feature health-food alternatives to junk foods, the newsletter mentioned above, browsing literature, or a vegetarian cooking contest with a prize to the winners and taste treats for everyone.

4. Have a vegetarian summer or winter party.

5. Write a letter to the editor or an article for a local paper on a health-related issue which affects your community.

6. Talk to local bookstores and libraries about increasing their stock of books and magazines that relate to vegetarianism.

7. If you have your own garden, share extra produce with friends or institutions such as homes for the elderly or the Salvation Army if they offer meals for the needy in your community. If you give vegetables to individuals or groups, include a vegetarian recipe or a list of related books available at your local bookstore or library.

Useful Resources

Baltimore Vegetarians (newsletter, other publications)
PO Box 1463
Baltimore, MD 21203
(301) 752-VEGV

Center for Science in the Public Interest
1757 S Street, NW
Washington, DC 20009

Community Food Education Program (teaching materials)
2606 Westwood Drive
Nashville, TN 37204
(615) 297-4088/4177

Educomics (Leonard Rifas)
Box 40246
San Francisco, CA 94140

Family Nutrition Newsletter
Deep Roots
606 Market St.
Lewisburg, PA 17837

Vegetarian Guide to Effective Use of the Mass Media
PO Box 5888
Bethesda, MD 20814

SCHOOL LUNCH 7

Once their child goes to school, parents face two problems: peer pressure from other children who think a vegetarian lunch is an oddity, and the level of nutrition in school lunches. Public schools and many day-care centers depend on resources provided by the federal and state governments. This reliance limits the variety and quality of menu choices to those foods allowable by government regulation and makes it somewhat more difficult to influence the food program of your child's school. Here are some comments and ideas from vegetarian parents about the issues surrounding school lunches:

"He prefers to buy his lunch because the other kids do and he doesn't want to stand out. In the public school he used to go to, he complained that he was the only child who brought sandwiches made out of whole wheat, so besides not wanting to be the only one who brings his lunch, he also doesn't want to show people that he has a different diet. I told him I wasn't about to go out and buy white bread; I would try to give him a few extra dessert items, something that might be a little more interesting to make up for the stigma of having whole wheat bread. I'd like to see him develop enough self-confidence so that he won't be ashamed of making proper nutritional choices."

Dan Hoffman, Ithaca, NY

"I pack lunches for them, which is definitely more expensive, but the food they serve at school is just not good. When he first started elementary school, Taio was getting all sorts of symptoms of hyperactivity: he had a constant itchy nose, big dark circles under his eyes, and he couldn't sit still. The school serves meat and a lot of refined bread, Jello and chemical ice cream—not high quality foods. All of the starches are refined. My kids have objected now and then to taking their own lunches when everybody else is buying, but they don't seem to mind too much. I pack things they like—fruit, kefir or yoghurt, nuts. I often give them rice cakes with a little butter and some Veg-Ex (a yeast extract), or a cheese sandwich, peanut butter and jam, sprouts.

"My son's day care was very good, they served natural foods, but the schools! When my kids were first there, I tried asking, 'Why don't we do something about this?' I was assuming that the meals were made in the school and that some of us could go in and have some influence. But this is not the case; the meals are all made in one big central place and shipped out to the schools. You're dealing with a centralized bureaucracy where meals are planned months ahead. There seems to be little parents can do. It's easier just to pack their lunches."

Jane Palomountain, Ithaca, NY

"Kristin, who's twelve, hates school lunches. It would be better if she could take her own lunch to school, but the lunch there is free, and that's a big factor now. Also, if she's going to take her own lunch, I want her to take the responsibility of making it, which she refuses to do. We've talked about having her take her lunch part of the time so that she can avoid the really bad lunches, but the things she is willing to take are all expensive, and I just don't have the money."

Becky Logan, Ithaca, NY

"Packing lunches was difficult; it was hard to give my daughter enough good food that she would eat so that she wouldn't want the junk foods. I used a lot of fresh vegetables and fruits and salads. At that point, a lot of the kids were spending the money they were given for lunches on potato chips and candy instead of lunches. In Massachusetts, several of us got together a petition to try to get the school to stop selling that stuff in the cafeteria, because that's all the kids were eating. The school lunches were so bad that the kids didn't want to eat them anyway. It was a real bind."

Rayne, Ithaca, NY

When my son entered a day-care center at age two, the high quality of care far outweighed the planned menu. His teachers knew he didn't eat meat; we kept a supply of peanut butter and tahini on hand as an alternative protein source, sometimes adding yoghurt or cheese. But overall, I felt that the meals were possibly adequate, but not great.

A few other parents felt the same way, and we met together to develop an alternative menu plan. The major problem turned out to be the cook, who had been working there for years, cooking with white sugar and white flour, etc., with the best of intentions. For example, she felt that children deserve sweets, that cookies and cake were part of what made childhood fun. Since she genuinely cared for the children, and firmly stuck to her beliefs, our request for a menu change was to her a personal affront. Changes took place, however, after the center surveyed parents about food preferences, and she had to face the fact that almost everyone else involved with the center felt differently than she did.

The new menu, which needed USDA approval, took a long time to be instated. The changes, although not radical, included the removal of puddings, cakes, and hot dogs, and the addition of whole wheat bread and rice cakes instead of white-flour baked goods. The majority of the meals became vegetarian (although not vegan). The new menu is not ideal by any means, but certainly a step in the right direction.

Here in Ithaca, the school-lunch director has incorporated whole grains into the menu along with more fruits and vegetables and less fat. Cost and availability of foods present problems. Products such as whole grains are bought at a state-wide level, and Ithaca is among only a very small number of New York State districts to request these foods.

Educational programs complement the changes in the lunchroom. In elementary schools especially there has been a good deal of hands-on experience with food. Volunteers, college students, and nutritionists in the community have worked with children from kindergarten through sixth grade, introducing them to new foods and teaching food preparation. The response of children in the classroom to a new recipe can cue the school lunch staff about whether or not to try it out on the whole school.

In 1980, *East-West Journal* ran an inspiring story about the Santa Cruz school-lunch program. Thelma Dalman, the program director, has kept it leaping forward since the early seventies, establishing the district's own whole-grain bakery, eliminating first chemical additives and then sugar, introducing a vegetarian alternative to the menu, while steadily increasing the variety and quality of foods served.

Much of the original impetus for these changes came when Dalman teamed up with Dr. Ben Feingold to do a study of the relationship of hyperactivity to food additives, with thirty-five Santa Cruz students participating. Parents and teachers were excited at the difference apparent in hyperactive children once they were no longer consuming additives. Dalman followed through by removing additives form lunches district-wide.

Again, the lunch program goes hand in hand with nutrition education. Vegetable Acceptance Campaigns encourage children to eat fresh vegetables, a nutritionist has been hired to educate both students and teachers, and a parent education program, with bilingual meetings, has begun.

Dalman's energy and commitment are backed primarily by the support of parents, not school personnel. This fact suggests that you may want to begin your own campaign among parents. Talk to the lunch-program director in your district as well, to see what changes she is willing to try. Sympathetic teachers may provide a way in, even if you begin by simply bringing healthy snacks every week or two. With support, something can be done.

There is a wealth of information for parents, school nutritionists, and teachers on incorporating nutritious natural foods into the school curriculum and lunch program. The following are some of the materials with which I am familiar and most highly recommend:

1. Bershad, Caro, and Deborah Bernick. *Bodyworks: The Kid's Guide to Food and Physical Fitness.* Random House, 1981. This book is designed for older children to use on their own—or, more realistically, as a workbook in the schools. It is not a vegetarian workbook, although it does examine the problems of eating meat, particularly as regards animals being the highest step in the food chain and therefore a much less economical food source. Without being vegetarian, the authors raise questions about the ill effects on our health of eating meat. The book is fun, easy to work with, and spiced with humor, thinking tests about fitness and nutrition, historical perspectives and facts on the foods we eat and how we eat them. The authors examine how our food beliefs affect our food choices.

2. Cohen, Leslie. *Nourishing a Happy Affair.* Larson Publications, 4936 Route 414, Burdett, NY 14818, 1983. This book, written for new vegetarians, has an *excellent* section on the author's involvement with the school-lunch program and reminds us all that things *can* be changed.

3. Exter, Pat. *The Lunchbox Book.* McBooks Press, 106 N. Aurora St., Ithaca, NY 14850, 1985. Written by a parent/teacher, this book is a valuable step-by-step parenting guide to providing

nutritious lunches. In addition to an excellent discussion on including children in the process of food planning and preparation, the author shares many tested lunchbox recipes and lunchpacking tips.

4. *Food Comix*. Educomics, Box 40246, San Francisco, CA 94140. This publication promotes food education through the comic-book format and is concerned with such issues as agribusiness, candy, caffeine, and the international nutrition scene. (#1 deals with Guatemala.)

5. Goodwin, Mary, and Gerry Pollen. *Creative Food Experiences for Children*. The Center for Science in the Public Interest, 1755 S St., NW, Washington, DC 20009, 1980. This is one of the most comprehensive books I have seen on the subject. The contents include: a detailed guide to involving children in vegetarian food experiences; suggestions for expanding a school food and nutrition curriculum; a comprehensive list of resources; ideas for lunches, snacks, and celebrations; and recipes. It is a practical, easy-to-use and well-researched book that I would recommend for every teacher in preschools and elementary schools.

6. Gribi, Gerri. "The Subversive Vegetarian: How to Get Wholesome Foods into Group Food Programs." *Vegetarian Times*, April 1982.

7. Mapes, Martha C. "G.U.L.P. An Alternate Method of Reaching Teens." *Journal of Nutrition Education* 9, no. 1 (Jan-March 1977). This article describes the results of a nutrition program based on a comic-book format, funded in part by a grant from the NY State College of Human Ecology for Public Services/Continuing Education.

Examples of Innovative School-Food Programs

Alameda, California
At Alameda High School, in what is known as the "Brown Bag Conspiracy," four teachers and twenty-five students gather weekly for a meal made entirely of natural foods.

Denver, Colorado
Public school-lunch programs feature freshly baked breads, fresh produce, meat entrees low in fat, and 2%-fat milk. A la carte alternatives include a vegetarian plate and do not offer junk foods. The program has in-service training for food service employees, nutrition education, and a student advisory council.

Smithtown, New York
An additive-free lunch especially designed for hyperactive children is available to any student upon request at no extra cost. Students have a choice of four, eight, or twelve entrees in elementary, intermediate, and secondary schools, respectively. One choice available to elementary students is selected weekly by one class in each school.

Harborfields, New York
Lunches in the Harborfields school district include whole, fresh foods and no junk foods. Food service workers attend semi-monthly training sessions. The physical education teacher and school nurse teach students about good foods. The program operates without subsidy from the district.

Conclusion

Although *Vegetarian Children* includes some recipe suggestions, it should not be thought of as a cookbook. Since over the past several years many excellent vegetarian cookbooks have been published, I didn't see the need to duplicate or reinvent recipes that are already easily available.

In *Vegetarian Children*, I chose to concentrate on aspects of vegetarianism that go beyond the limits of a cookbook and address not only health and nutrition, but also the broader social and moral issues that are closely connected with vegetarianism. I do think, however, that a good source of recipes is invaluable when trying to offer our families healthful and tasty meals. The following is a list of some of the many cookbooks available—old favorites and new—that might help you to add variety and good nutrition to your meals.

Abehsera, Michel. *Zen Macrobiotic Cooking.* New York: Avon, 1968.

Bauer, Cathy, and Juel Anderson. *The Tofu Cookbook.* Emmaus, PA: Rodale Press, 1979.

Brown, Edward. *Tassajara Cooking.* Boulder, CO: Shambala Publ., 1986.

Colbin, Annemarie. *The Book of Whole Meals.* New York: Ballantine, 1979.

Cusumano, Camille. *Tofu, Tempeh, and Other Soy Delights.* Emmaus, PA: Rodale Press, 1984.

Elliot Rose. *The Vegetarian Mother Baby Book.* New York: Random House, 1986.

Ewald, Ellen Buchman. *Recipes for a Small Planet.* New York: Ballantine, 1973.

Esko, Wendy. *Introducing Macrobiotic Cooking.* New York: Japan Publications, 1981.

Kidder, Lew, ed. *Uprisings: Whole Grain Bakers' Book.* New York: Bantam, 1983.

Mayo, Patricia Terris. *Sugarless Baking Book.* Boulder, CO: Shambala Publ., 1979.

Robertson, Laurel, et al. *The New Laurel's Kitchen.* Berkeley, CA: Ten Speed Press, 1986.

_____ . *Laurel's Kitchen Bread Book.* New York: Random House, 1984.

Sams, Craig and Ann. *The Brown Rice Cookbook.* New York: Thorsons Publishers, 1983.

Shulman, Martha Rose. *Fast Vegetarian Feasts.* New York: Doubleday, 1982.

Bibliography

Altman, Nathaniel. "Revising the Basic Four." *Vegetarian Times*, Sept./Oct. 1977.

Ames, Louise Bates, et al. *The Gesell Institute's Child from One to Six*. New York: Harper and Row, 1979.

Arasaki, Seiben and Ternko. *Vegetables from the Sea*. New York: Japan Publications, 1983.

Archard, Merry. *Cook for Your Kids*. New York: Grove Press, 1975.

Aronson, E., and J. M. Carlsmith. "Effect of Severity of Threat on the Devaluation of Forbidden Behavior." *J. Abn. Soc. Psych.* 66 (1963): 584-588.

Ault, Roz, and Liz Uranek. *Kids are Natural Cooks*. Boston: Houghton Mifflin Co., 1974.

Bachrach, S., et al. "An Outbreak of Vitamin D Deficiency Rickets on a Susceptible Population." *Pediatrics* 64 (1979): 871-877.

Bard, Bernard. *The School Lunchroom: Time of Trial*. New York: John Wiley and Sons, 1968.

Beauchamp, G., and O. Maller. "The Development of Flavor Preferences in Humans: A Review." *In The Chemical Senses and Nutrition*, ed. R. Kare and O. Maller. New York: Academic Press, 1977.

Bell, A. Chris, et al. "A Method for Describing Food Beliefs Which May Predict Personal Food Choices." *J. Nutr. Ed.* 13, no. 1 (1981): 22-25.

Bergen, James G., and P. T. Brown. "Nutritional Status of the 'New' Vegetarians." *J. Am. Diet. Assoc.* 76 (1980): 151-155.

Berkelhamer, J. E., et al. "Kwashiorkor in Chicago." *Am. J. Dis. Child* 129 (1975): 1240.

Bershad, Carol, and Deborah Bernick. *Bodyworks: The Kids' Guide to Physical Fitness.* New York: Random House, 1979.

Birch, L.L. "Dimensions of Children's Food Preferences." *J. Nutr. Ed.* 11, no. 4 (1979): 77-80.

_____ . "Preschool Children's Food Preference and Consumption Patterns." *J. Nutri. Ed.* 11, no. 4 (1979): 189-192.

Birch, L. L., et al. "The Influence of Social-Affective Context on the Formation of Children's Food Preferences." *J. Nutr. Ed.* 13, no. 1 (1981): 115-118.

Bossard, J. H. S., and E. S. Boll. *Sociology of Child Development.* 4th ed. New York: Harper and Row, 1966.

Bradford, Peter and Montse. *Cooking with Sea Vegetables.* London: Thorsons Pubs., 1985.

Braunstein, Mark Matthew. *Radical Vegetarianism.* Los Angeles: Panjandrum Books, 1981.

Breckenridge, M. E. "Food Attitudes of Five to Twelve Year Old Children." *J. Am. Diet. Assoc.* 35 (1959): 704-709.

Brown, P. T., and J. G. Bergen. "Dietary Status of 'New' Vegetarians." *J. Amer. Diet. Assoc.* 67 (1975): 455-459.

Burt, J. V., and A. A. Hertzler. "Parental Influence on the Child's Food Preference." *J. Nutri. Ed.* 10 (1978): 127-128.

Cabanac, M. "The Physiological Role of Pleasantness." *Science* 173 (1971): 1103-1107.

Caplan, Theresa and Frank. *The Early Childhood Years*. New York: Perigree Books, 1983.

Chery, A., and J. H. Sabry. "Portion size of Common Foods Eaten by Young Children." *J. Can. Diet. Assoc.* 45 (1984): 230-233.

Children's Foundation. "Eating Better at School: An Organizer's Guide." Washington, DC: Center for Science in the Public Interest, 1980.

Coffin, Lewis A. *Children's Nutrition: A Consumer's Guide*. Santa Barbara: Capra Press, 1984.

Cohen, Stanley A. *Healthy Babies, Happy Kids*. New York: Delilah Books, 1982.

Cohen, Y. A. "Food and its Vicissitudes: A Cross-Cultural Study of Sharing and Non-Sharing." In *Social Structure and Personality*, ed. Cohen, Y. A. New York: Holt, Rinehart and Winston, 1961.

Colbin, Annemarie. "Children and Junk Food." *East West Journal*, Sept. 1982.

Contento, I. "Children's Thinking About Food and Eating—A Piagetian-based Study." *J. Nutr. Ed.* 13, no. 1 (1981): 86-90.

Crespi, Vicki. *Journal of Raising a Vegetarian Child*. New York: Broken Hour Press.

Cunningham, Jo Lynn, et al. "Development of CANKAP—A Multidimensional Measure of Nutritional Belief." *J. Nutr. Ed.* 13, No. 3 (1981): 109-114.

Daniel-Gentry, Jean, et al. "Increasing the Use of Meatless Meals." *J. Am. Diet. Assoc.* 86, no. 6 (1986): 778-781.

Day, Nancy Raines. *Help Yourself to Health*. New York: New Readers Press, 1980.

Dehr, Roma. *A Fable for Vegetarian Children: The Story of Thor*. Vancouver, BC: Namchi United Enterprises, 1981.

Denzin, Norman K. *Childhood Socialization*. San Francisco: Jossey-Bass, 1977.

DePaola, D. P., et al. "Diet and Oral Health." In *Sourcebook on Food and Nutrition*, eds. Scarpa, I. S., et al. Chicago: Marquis Academic Media, 1980.

Dept. of Health, Education and Welfare. *Nutrition Education for Young Children*. DHEW Publication no. 76-31015. Washington, DC, 1976.

Dept. of Health, Education and Welfare. *Nutritional Disorders of Children*. DHEW Publication no. 77-5104. Washington, DC, 1977.

Douglas, Mary. "Accounting for Taste." *Psychology Today*, July 1979.

Dowie, Mark, et al. "The Illusion of Safety." *Mother Jones*, June 1982.

Dreikurs, Rudolf. *Children the Challenge*. New York: Hawthorn Books, 1964.

_____ . *The Challenge of Parenthood*. New York: Hawthorn Books, 1958.

Dufty, William. *Sugar Blues*. New York: Warner Books, 1976.

Duncker, K. "Experimental Modification of Children's Food Preferences Through Social Suggestion". *J. Abn. Soc. Psych.* 33 (1938): 489-507.

Duska, Ronald, and M. Whelan. *Moral Development: A Guide to Piaget and Kohlberg*. New York: Paulist Press, 1975.

Dwyer, Johanna T., et al. "Growth in 'New' Vegetarian Preschool Children Using the Jenss-Bayley Curve Fitting Technique." *Am. J. Clin. Nutr.* 37 (1983): 815-827.

_____ . "Mental Age and IQ of Predominantly Vegetarian Children." *J. Am. Diet. Assoc.* 76 (1980): 142-147.

_____ . "Nutritional Status of Vegetarian Children." *Am. J. Clin. Nutr.* 35 (1982): 204-216.

_____ . "Preschoolers on Alternate Lifestyle Diets." *J. Am. Diet. Assoc.* 72 (1978): 264-270.

_____ . "Risk of Nutrition Rickets Among Vegetarian Children." *Am. J. Dis. Child* 133 (1979): 134-140.

_____ . "Size, Obesity and Leanness in Vegetarian Preschool Children." *J. Am. Diet. Assoc.* 77 (1980): 434-439.

Eide, Wenche Barth. "The Nutrition Educator's Role in Access to Food—From Individual Orientation to Social Orientation." *J. Nutr. Ed.* 14, no. 1 (1982): 14-17.

Eppright, Ercel, et al. "Eating Behavior of Preschool Children." *J. Nutr. Ed.* 13, no. 3 (Summer Supplement 1969).

Farber, C. *Sweet Dreams: A Story About Healthy Eating.* New York: Siroca Productions, 1978.

Fischer, Kim. "A Child is More than a Stomach." *Mothering,* Winter 1983.

Ford, Richard, and Juel and Sigrid Anderson. *Juel Anderson's Sea Green Primer.* Berkely: Creative Arts Book Co., 1983.

Fraiberg, Selma. *The Magic Years.* New York: Charles Scribner's Sons, 1959.

Freedman, J. L. "Long Term Behavioral Effects of Cognitive Dissonance." *J. Exper. Psych.* 1 (1965): 145-155.

Freedland-Graves, J. H., et al. "Nutrition Knowledge of Vegetarians and Non-Vegetarians." *J. Nutr. Ed.* 14 (1982): 21-25.

Fulton, J. R., et al. "Preschool Vegetarian Children." *J. Am. Diet. Assoc.* 76 (1981): 360-365.

Gibson, Lawrence D. "Psychology of Food: Why We Eat What We Eat When We Eat." *Food Technology* 35 (1981): 54-56.

Gilligan, Carol. *In a Different Voice.* Cambridge: Harvard University Press, 1982.

Gooch, Sandy. *If You Love Me, Don't Feed Me Junk!* Reston, VA: Reston Publishing Co., 1983.

Goodwin, Mary T., and Gerry Pollen. *Creative Food Experiences for Children.* Washington, DC: Center for Science in the Public Interest, 1980.

Gribbi, Gerri. "The Subversive Vegetarian: How to Get Wholesome Foods into Group Food Programs." *Vegetarian Times,* April 1982.

Graitcher, P. L., and E. M. Gentry. "Measuring Children: One Reference for All." *Lancet* 2 (1981): 297-299.

Haas, Ellen. *Children's Advertising: Legislative Testimony and Exhibits of the Community Nutrition Institute.* Washington, DC: Community Nutrition Institute, 1978.

Habicht, J., et al. "Height and Weight Standards for Preschool Children: How Relevant are Ethnic Differences in Growth Potential?" *Lancet* 1 (1974): 611-615.

Hartbarger, J. C. and N. J. *Eating for the Eighties.* New York: Holt, Rinehart and Winston, 1981.

Hatch, Sandra. "Sugar and Dental Caries." *Family Perspective* 15 (1981): 25-32.

Hatfield, Antoinette Kuzmanich, and Peggy Smeeton Stanton. *How to Help Your Child Eat Right.* Washington, DC: Acropolis Books, 1978.

Herbert, J. R., and C. Waternaux. "Graphical Displays of Growth Data." *Am. J. Clin. Nutr.* 38, no. 1 (1983): 145-147.

Hebert, James R. "Relationship of Vegetarianism to Child Growth in South India." *Am. J. Clin. Nutr.* 42 (1985): 1246-1254.

Hertzler, Ann A. "Classifying Cultural Food Habits and Meanings." *J. Am. Diet. Assoc.* 80, no. 5 (1982): 421-425.

_____ . "Development of an Iron Checklist to Guide Food Intake." *J. Am. Diet. Assoc.* 86, no. 6 (1986): 782-785.

Hewitt, Karen. *The Kitchen Book: Notes from a Child Care Center.* Vermont: Queen City Printers, 1978.

Higginbottom, M. C., et al. "A Syndrome of Methylmalonic Aciduria, Homocystinuria, Megaloblastic Anemia and Neurologic Abnormalities in a Vitamin B12 Deficient Breast-Fed Infant of a Strict Vegetarian." *New England Journal of Medicine* 299 (1978): 317-323.

Hunter, Beatrice Trum. "Food or Fake, You Can't Tell the Difference, or Can You?" *Health Quarterly,* Nov./Dec. 1980.

Ingrasci, Rick, and Carol Englender. "Caution: Herbs May be Harmful." *New Age Journal,* April 1981.

Jelliffe, D. *Infant Nutrition in Subtropics and Tropics.* 2nd. ed. World Health Organization, Monograph no. 29. 1968.

Jerome, N. W., ed. *Dimensions of Nutrition.* Boulder: Colorado Associated Univ. Pr., 1969.

John, T. J., et al. "Kwashiorkor not Associated with Poverty." *J. Pediat,* 90 (1977): 730-735.

Kamen, Betty and Si. *Kids are What They Eat.* New York: Avco Publications, 1983.

Kennedy, Sheila, and Susan Seidman. *Working Family's Kitchen Guide.* San Francisco: 101 Productions, 1980.

Keville, Kathi. "How to make Tooth Powder, Toothpaste, and Mouthwash." *Vegetarian Times,* Jan. 1982.

Kohl, Herbert. *Growing with Your Children.* Boston: Little, Brown, 1978.

Kohlberg, L., and R. Kramer. "Continuities and Discontinuities in Childhood and Adult Moral Development." *Human Development* 12 (1969): 93-120.

Kohlberg, Lawrence. *The Philosophy of Moral Development.* San Francisco: Harper and Row, 1981.

Kraus, Ruth, and Crockett Johnson. *The Carrot Seed.* New York: Scholastic Books, 1945.

Kruesi, Markus. "Carbohydrate Intake and Children's Behavior." *Food Technology,* Jan. 1980.

Kushi, Aveline and Michio. *Macrobiotic Family Favorites: Cooking for Healthy Children.* Briarcliff Manor, NY: Japan Publications, 1979.

Kushi, Michio and Aveline. *Macrobiotic Child Care and Family Health.* Briarcliff Manor, NY: Japan Publications, 1979.

Lane, Carolyn, and Pamela Zapata. *The Mother's Cook and Cope Book.* New York: Viking Press, 1972.

Lansky, Vicki. *The Taming of the C.A.N.D.Y. Monster.* Deephaven, MN: Meadowbrook Press, 1978.

Laude, Nathaniel, and Afton Slade. *Stages.* San Francisco: Harper and Row, 1979.

Lawless, Harry. "Sensory Development in Children." *J. Am. Diet. Assoc.* 85, no. 5 (1985): 577-582.

Leach, Penelope. *The Child Care Encyclopedia.* New York: Alfred A. Knopf, 1984.

Lee, Thomas R., et al. "Nutritional Understanding of Preschool Children Taught in the Home or a Child Development Laboratory." *Home Economics Research Journal* 13, no. 1 (1984): 52-60.

Lowenberg, M. E. "Food Preferences of Young Children." *J. Am. Diet. Assoc.* 24 (1948): 430-434.

_____ . "The Development of Food Patterns." *J. Am. Diet. Assoc.* 65 (1974): 263-268.

_____ . "The Development of Food Patterns in Young Children." In *Nutrition in Infancy and Childhood*, ed. Peggy L. Pipes. St. Louis, MO: C. V. Mosby, 1977.

Lowenberg, M. E., and M. Bryan. "The Father's Influence on Young Children's Food Preferences." *J. Am. Diet. Assoc.* 31 (1958): 30.

Lynch, Harold D. *Your Child is What He Eats.* Chicago: Henry Regnery Co., 1958.

MacLean, W. C., and G. G. Graham. "Vegetarianism in Children." *Am. J. Dis. Child* 134 (1980): 513-519.

Maller, O., and J. A. Desor. "Effect of Taste on Ingestion by Human Newborns." In *Fourth Symposium on Oral Sensation and Perception.* Washington: GPO, 1973.

Mapes, Martha C. "An Alternative Method of Reaching Teens." *J. Nutr. Info.* 9 (1977): 12-16.

Marquiles, Jane U., and E. Kaufman. *The Healthy Family Cookbook.* New York: Harper and Row, 1974.

Martin, Ethel, and Virginia Beal. *Robert's Nutrition Work with Children.* 4th ed. Illinois: University of Chicago, 1978.

Martin, Judith. *Miss Manners' Guide to Rearing Perfect Children.* New York: Penguin Books, 1985.

Maschette, Diane. "Moral Reasoning in the 'Real World!'" *Theory into Practice* 2 (1977): 124-128.

McFadden, Michael. *Bachelor Fatherhood.* New York: Walker and Co., 1974.

McKee, Trevor. "Three Faces of Moral Development: Conscience, Moral Reasoning and Moral Behavior." *Family Perspective* 9 (1975): 37-44.

Mendelsohn, Robert S. *How to Raise a Healthy Child in Spite of Your Doctor.* Chicago: Contemporary Books, 1984.

Mitchell, K. J. "A Kohlbergian Assessment of Young Children's Moral Development." Thesis, Cornell University, 1981.

Morley, John, and A. Levine. "The Central Control of Appetite." *Lancet,* Feb. 1983. 398-401.

Moyer, Anne. *Better Food for Public Places.* Emmaus, PA: Rodale Press, 1977.

Mullis, R. L. "Parental Behaviors and Moral Judgements in First Grade Children." *Family Perspective* 15 (1981): 35-41.

National Research Council. *Recommended Dietary Allowances.* 9th ed. Washington, DC: NRC, 1980.

National School Lunch Program. *Food Consumption and Nutrition Evaluation.* Washington, DC: Food and Nutrition Service, 1979.

Natow, Annette, and Jo-Ann Heslin. *No-Nonsense Nutrition for Kids.* New York: McGraw Hill, 1985.

Norwood, Christopher. *At Highest Risk.* New York: Penguin Books, 1980.

Osuhor, P. C. "Weaning Practices Amongst the Hausas." *J. Human Nutrition* 34 (1980): 273-280.

Papert, Seymour. *Mindstorms,* New York: Basic Books, 1980.

Pearce, Joseph. *Magical Child.* New York: Dutton, 1977.

Peterkin, Betty. "The RDA or U.S. RDA?" *J. Nutr. Ed.* 9, no. 1 (1977): 10-11.

Phillips, B. K., and K. K. Kolasa. "Vegetable Preferences of Preschoolers in Day Care." *J. Nutr. Ed.* 12 (1980): 192-195.

Pipes, Peggy L. *Nutrition in Infancy and Childhood.* St. Louis, MO: C. V. Mosby, 1977.

————— . "Assessing Food and Nutrient Intake." In *Assessment and Management of Development Change and Problems in Children.* 2d ed., St. Louis, MO: C. V. Mosby, 1981.

Powers, Hugh, and James Presley. *Food Power: Nutrition and Your Child's Behavior.* New York: St. Martin's Press, 1978.

Purves, R. "Vegan Diets for Young Children." *Nutrition and Food Science,* Jan./Feb. 1981.

Raman, S. P. "Role of Nutrition in the Actualization of Potentialities of the Child." *Young Children* 31 (1975): 24-32.

Read, Marsha, and Diane Thomas. "Nutrient and Food Supplement Practices of Lacto-Ovo-Vegetarians." *J. Am. Diet. Assoc.* 82 (1983): 403-407.

Richards, Mary L. "Food and Nutrition Education in American Elementary Schools." *J. Consumer Studies and Home Economics* 9 (1985): 327-340.

Ripault, Christine, and C. Turgeon. eds. *Children's Gastronomique.* New York: Crown, 1968.

Robertson, Laurel, et al. *Laurel's Kitchen: A Handbook for Vegetarian Cookery and Nutrition.* California: Nilgiri Press, 1976.

Robichaux, Faye, and Sam Adams. "Offer vs. Serve Food Service in Lower Elementary School Lunchrooms." *J. Am. Diet. Assoc.* 85 (1985): 853-854.

Robson, J. R. K. "Zen Macrobiotic Dietary Problems in Infancy." *Pediatrics* 53 (1974): 326-329.

Rozin, Paul, et al. "The Child's Conception of Food: The Development of Categories of Acceptable and Rejected Substances." *J. Nutr. Ed.* 18, no. 2 (1986): 75-81.

Rubin, Zick. "Does Personality Really Change After Twenty?" *Psychology Today*, May 1981.

Sadalla, Edward, and Jeffry Burroughs. "Profiles in Eating: Sexy Vegetarians and Other Diet-Based Social Stereotypes." *Psychology Today*, Oct. 1981.

Sanders, T. A. B., and R. Purves. "An Anthropometric and Dietary Assessment of the Nutritional Status of Vegan Preschool Children." *J. Human Nutrition* 35 (1981): 349-357.

Satler, Ellyn M. "Childhood Eating Disorders." *J. Am. Diet. Assoc.* 86, no. 3 (1986): 357-361.

_____ . "The Feeding Relationship." *J. Am. Diet. Assoc.* 86, no. 3 (1986): 352-356.

Scarpa, I. S., et al. *Sourcebook on Food and Nutrition*. Chicago: Marquis Academic Media, 1980.

Shandler, Michael and Nina. *Raising Your Child as a Vegetarian*. New York: Schocken, 1981.

Shull, M., et al. "Seasonal Variations in Preschool Vegetarian Children's Growth Velocities." *Am. J. Clin. Nutr.* 31 (1978): 1-2.

_____ . "Velocities of Growth in Vegetarian Preschool Children." *Pediatrics* 60 (1977): 410-417.

Singer, Eliot A. "Folklore for Nutrition Education." *J. Nutr. Ed.* 14, no. 1 (1982): 12-13.

Strobl, C., and L. Groll. "Professional Knowledge and Attitudes on Vegetarianism: Implications for Practice." *J. Am. Diet. Assoc.* 79 (1981): 568-574.

Trahms, C. M. "Dietary Patterns of Vegans, Vegetarians and Non-Vegetarian Preschool Children." *Soc. Nutr. Ed. Commun.* 6 (1975): 13.

_____ . "Vegetarian Diets for Children." In *Nutrition in Infancy and Child-hood*, ed. Peggy Pipes. St. Louis, MO: C. V. Mosby Co., 1977.

Truesdell, Delores, and Phyllis Acosta. "Feeding the Vegan Infant and Child." *J. Am. Diet. Assoc.* 85 (1985): 837-840.

Tsuji, Shizuo. *Japanese Cooking: A Simple Art.* New York: Kodansha, 1982.

Turner, E., and J. C. Wright. "Effects of Severity of Threat and Perceived Availability on the Attractiveness of Objects." *Journal of Personality and Social Psychology* 2 (1965): 128-132.

US Department of Agriculture. *1979 USDA Yearbook: What's to Eat and Other Questions Kids Ask About Food.* Washington, DC: GPO, 1979.

Van Matre, Steve. *Acclimatizing.* Martinsville, In: American Camping Association, 1974.

Van Staveren, Wija, et al. "Food Consumption and Height/Weight Status of Dutch Preschool Children on Alternative Diets." *J. Am. Diet. Assoc.* 85, no. 12 (1985): 1579-1584.

Vyhmeister, I. B., et al. "Safe Vegetarian Diets for Children." *Pediat. Clin. N.A.* 24 (1977): 203-206.

Wagner, Martha. "Kids in the Kitchen". *New Age Journal*, Jan. 1981.

_____. "Learning to Love Seaweed." *New Age Journal*, April 1981.

Wallace, Maureen and Jim. *Kick the Junk Food Habit with Snackers.* Seattle, WA: Madrona Publications, 1978.

Wasserman, D., and C. Stahler. *I Love Animals and Broccoli.* Maryland: Baltimore Vegetarians, 1985.

Weiffenbach, James. *Taste and Development.* Washington, DC: GPO, 1977.

Weiner, Michael A. *The Art of Feeding Children Well.* New York: Warner Books, 1982.

Weiss, Patricia Suarez. "A View Behind the Scenes of Pinwheel." *Vegetarian Times*, Jan. 1982.

Whiting, Beatrice B. *Six Cultures: Studies of Child Rearing*. New York: John Wiley and Sons, 1963.

Wilkinson, J. F. "How to Get Your Kids to Eat Less Without Dieting." *Health Quarterly*, Nov./Dec. 1980.

Wilson, Christine, ed. "Supplement 1: Food—Custom and Nurture." *Jr. Nutr. Ed.* 11 (1979): 4.

Worthington-Roberts, Bonnie. *Contemporary Developments in Nutrition*. St. Louis, MO: C. V. Mosby, 1981.

Wynder, Ernest L., ed. *The Book of Health*, New York: Franklin Watts, 1981.

Younathan, Margaret, et al. "Food Patterns of Two-Parent, Two-Child Households of Urban South Louisiana." *Journal of Consumer Studies and Home Economics* 9 (1985): 221-235.

Zmora, E., et al. "Multiple Nutritional Deficiencies in Infants from a Strict Vegetarian Community." *Am. J. Dis. Child* 133 (1979): 141-144.

Index

By the author of *Vegetarian Children:*

Vegetarian Baby
by Sharon Yntema

Now in an eighth, updated printing, **Vegetarian Baby** is acknowledged to be the definitive sourcebook for parents who want to raise their child on a nutritionally complete, meatless diet. Valuable charts and tables accompany essential nutrition information for the pregnant mother and the growing child. Interviews with vegetarian parents provide reassuring insights for new parents. Ms. Yntema discusses a wide range of diets including vegan, lacto-ova, Fruitarian, and macrobiotic, and offers many practical suggestions on food preparation and recipes for healthy vegetarian babies.

I think this book is great. The author has extensively researched and documented the topic she covers, and yet presents them in a relaxed and easy to read style. The information she offers is current, accurate, and extensive: It will give parents the knowledge and confidence necessary to raise their child on a meatless diet.
—Vegetarian Times

Much more than a cookbook and a nutritional guide, VEGETARIAN BABY *also deals with child development and food attitudes. And it's delightfully readable—wish I'd had it when I was pregnant with my daughter.*
—Medical Self Care

Sensible, intelligent, well-researched, and documented, as well as practical... unsurpassed by any other currently available volume... highly recommended.
—Library Journal

The book is a needed response to critics and a sourcebook for parents. —Mothering

$8.95 paper
ISBN 0-935526-02-1
illustrations, line drawings, charts, and tables; 5½" x 8½"; 224 pages

——— **also available from McBooks Press** ———

Check your favorite bookstore for other McBooks Press books.
(Or use this form to order directly.)

McBooks Press
908 Steam Mill Road
Ithaca, NY 14850

Name _____

Address _____

_____

City _____ State _____ Zip _____

Quantity	Title	Price	Total
_____	Finger Lakes Wineries, 2nd (Wiener)	12.95	_____
_____	From Blood to Verdict (Homsher)	12.95	_____
_____	Lunchbox Book (Exter)	7.95	_____
_____	Raccoon Book (Aal)	5.95	_____
_____	Restaurant Gde. to the Finger Lakes, 2nd	8.95	_____
_____	A Sense of Place (Clardy, editor)	9.95	_____
_____	Vegetarian Baby (Yntema)	8.95	_____
_____	Vegetarian Children (Yntema)	8.95	_____
_____	The Wings, the Vines (Aal et. al.)	6.50	_____

Subtotal _____

Shipping & Handling + 1.35

Subtotal _____

8% tax (NYS only) _____

Total Enclosed _____

Please enclose your check or money order. Thank you.